BOOKS BY MR. STEDMAN

PROSE AND POETIC WORKS. Including Poems, Victorian Poets, Poets of America, Nature and Elements of Poetry. 4 vols. uniform, crown 8vo, gilt top, in box, $7.50.

POEMS. *Household Edition.* With Portrait and Illustrations. 12mo, $1.50; full gilt, $2.00.

HAWTHORNE, AND OTHER POEMS. 16mo, $1.25.

VICTORIAN POETS. Revised and Enlarged Edition. Crown 8vo, gilt top, $2.25.

POETS OF AMERICA. A companion volume to "Victorian Poets." Crown 8vo, gilt top, $2.25.

THE NATURE AND ELEMENTS OF POETRY. Crown 8vo, gilt top, $1.50.

A VICTORIAN ANTHOLOGY. 1837–1895. Selections illustrating the Editor's Critical Review of British Poetry in the Reign of Victoria. Large 8vo, gilt top, $2.50; full gilt, $3.00.

POEMS NOW FIRST COLLECTED. 12mo, gilt top, $1.50.

AN AMERICAN ANTHOLOGY. Selections illustrating the Editor's Critical Review of Poetry in America. Large 8vo. (*In Preparation.*)

HOUGHTON, MIFFLIN AND COMPANY

BOSTON AND NEW YORK

POEMS
NOW FIRST COLLECTED

POEMS NOW FIRST COLLECTED: By EDMUND CLARENCE STEDMAN

BOSTON: HOUGHTON, MIFFLIN AND COMPANY: *NEW YORK*

MDCCCXCVII

COPYRIGHT 1897
BY EDMUND CLARENCE STEDMAN
ALL RIGHTS RESERVED

TO MY WIFE

CONTENTS

I

VARIOUS POEMS

II

OTHER SONGS AND BALLADS

III

COMMEMORATIONS

IV

THE CARIB SEA

V

ARIEL

NOTE — Having delayed collecting my own poems of recent years, I now find them so various in theme, motive, and expression as to render their arrangement a somewhat difficult task. The plan finally adopted seems as good as any other. With few exceptions, the pieces within each of the general divisions are given in the order of their composition as shown by the respective dates. The Caribbean series has been completed for this volume, and much of it appears for the first time.

E. C. S.

Thou, — whose endearing hand once laid in sooth
Upon thy follower, no want thenceforth,
Nor toil, nor joy and pain, nor waste of years
Filled with all cares that deaden and subdue,
Can make thee less to him — can make thee less
Than sovereign queen, his first liege, and his last
Remembered to the unconscious dying hour, —
Return and be thou kind, bright Spirit of song,
Thou whom I yet loved most, loved most of all
Even when I left thee — I, now so long strayed
From thy beholding! And renew, renew
Thy gift to me fain clinging to thy robe!
Still be thou kind, for still thou wast most dear.

1897

I

VARIOUS POEMS

MUSIC AT HOME

I SAT beneath a fragrant tasselled tree,
Whose trunk encoiling vines had made to be
A glossy fount of leafage. Sweet the air,
Far-off the smoke-veiled city and its care,
Precious and near the book within my hand —
The deathless song of that immortal land
Wherefrom Keats took his young Endymion
And laurelled bards enow their wreaths have
won; —
When from some topmost spray began to chant
And flute, and trill, a warbling visitant,
A cat-bird, riotous the world above,
Hasting to spend his heritage ere love
Should music change to madness in his throat,
Leaving him naught but one discordant note.
And as my home-bred chorister outvied
The nightingale, old England's lark beside,
I thought — What need to borrow? Lustier clime
Than ours Earth has not, — nor her scroll a time
Ampler of human glory and desire
To touch the plume, the brush, the lips, with fire;

MUSIC AT HOME

No sunrise chant on ancient shore and sea,
Since sang the morning stars, more worth shall be
Than ours, once uttered from the very heart
Of the glad race that here shall act its part.
Blithe prodigal, the rhythm free and strong
Of thy brave voice forecasts our poet's song!

THE HAND OF LINCOLN

Look on this cast, and know the hand
  That bore a nation in its hold:
From this mute witness understand
  What Lincoln was, — how large of mould

The man who sped the woodman's team,
  And deepest sunk the ploughman's share,
And pushed the laden raft astream,
  Of fate before him unaware.

This was the hand that knew to swing
  The axe — since thus would Freedom train
Her son — and made the forest ring,
  And drove the wedge, and toiled amain.

Firm hand, that loftier office took,
  A conscious leader's will obeyed,
And, when men sought his word and look,
  With steadfast might the gathering swayed.

THE HAND OF LINCOLN

No courtier's, toying with a sword,
  Nor minstrel's, laid across a lute;
A chief's, uplifted to the Lord
  When all the kings of earth were mute!

The hand of Anak, sinewed strong,
  The fingers that on greatness clutch;
Yet, lo! the marks their lines along
  Of one who strove and suffered much.

For here in knotted cord and vein
  I trace the varying chart of years;
I know the troubled heart, the strain,
  The weight of Atlas — and the tears.

Again I see the patient brow
  That palm erewhile was wont to press;
And now 't is furrowed deep, and now
  Made smooth with hope and tenderness.

For something of a formless grace
  This moulded outline plays about;
A pitying flame, beyond our trace,
  Breathes like a spirit, in and out, —

THE HAND OF LINCOLN

The love that cast an aureole
   Round one who, longer to endure,
Called mirth to ease his ceaseless dole,
   Yet kept his nobler purpose sure.

Lo, as I gaze, the statured man,
   Built up from yon large hand, appears:
A type that Nature wills to plan
   But once in all a people's years.

What better than this voiceless cast
   To tell of such a one as he,
Since through its living semblance passed
   The thought that bade a race be free!

1883

NOCTURNE

THE silent world is sleeping,
  And spirits hover nigh,
With downward pinions keeping
  Our love from mortal eye,
Nor any ear of Earth can hear
  The heart-beat and the sigh.

Now no more the twilight bird
  Showers his triple notes around;
In the dewy paths is heard
  No rude footfall's sound.
In the stillness I await
  Thy coming late,
In the dusk would lay my heart
Close to thine own, and say how dear thou art!

O life! O rarest hour!
  When the dark world onward rolls,
And the fiery planets drift,
  Then from our commingled souls

NOCTURNE

Clouds of passion and of power,
  Flames of incense, lift!

Come, for the world is turning
  To meet the morning star!
Answer my spirit's yearning
  And seek the arms that call thee from afar:
Let them close — ah, let them close
Around thee now, and lure thee to repose.

1878

"Ye Tombe of Ye Poet Chaucer"

Abbot and monks of Westminster
Here placed his tomb, in all men's view.
"Our Chaucer dead?" — King Harry said, —
"A mass for him, and burial due!"
This very aisle his footsteps knew;
Here Gower's benediction fell, —
Brother thou were and minstral trewe;
Now slepe thou wel.

There died with that old century's death,
I wot, five hundred years ago,
One whose blithe heart, whose morning art,
Made England's Castaly to flow.
He in whose song that fount we know,
With every tale the skylarks tell,
Had right, Saint Bennet's wall below
To slumber well.

Eftsoons his master piously
In Surrey hied him to his rest;

The Thames, between their closes green,
  Parted these warblers breast from breast, —
  The gravest from the joyfulest
Whose notes the matin chorus swell:
  A league divided, east and west,
    They slumber well.

Is there no care in holy ground
  The world's deep undertone to hear?
Can this strong sleep our Chaucer keep
  When May-time buds and blossoms peer?
  Less strange that many a sceptred year,
While the twin houses towered and fell,
  Alike through England's pride and fear,
    He slumbered well.

The envious Roses woefully
  By turns a bleeding kingdom sway;
Thrones topple down, — to robe and crown
  Who comes at last must hew his way.
  No sound of all that piteous fray,
Nor of its ceasing, breaks the spell;
  Still on, to great Eliza's day,
    He slumbers well.

Methinks, had Shakespeare lightly walked
  Anear him in the minster old,
He would have heard, — his sleep had stirred
  With dreams of wonders manifold;
  Even though no sad vibration told
His ear when sounded Mary's knell, —
  Though, when the mask on Charles laid hold,
    He slumbered well.

In climes beyond his calendar
  The latest century's splendors grow;
London is great, — the Abbey's state
  A young world's eager wanderers know;
  New songs, new minstrels, come and go;
Naught as of old outside his cell, —
  Just as of old, within it low,
    He slumbers well.

And now, when hawthorn is in flower,
  And throstles sing as once sang he,
In this last age, on pilgrimage
  Like mine from lands that distant be,
  Come youths and maidens, summer-free,
Where shades of bards and warriors dwell,
  And say, "The sire of minstrelsy
    Here slumbers well;"

And say, "While London's Abbey stands
  No less shall England's strength endure!"
Ay, though its old wall crumbling fall,
  Shall last her song's sweet overture;
  Some purling stream shall flow, be sure,
From out the ivied heap, to tell
  That here the fount of English pure
    Long slumbered well.

1879

THE CONSTANT HEART

SADDE songe is out of season
  When birdes and lovers mate,
When soule to soule must paye swete toll
  And fate be joyned with fate;
Sadde songe and wofull thought controle
  This constant heart of myne,
And make newe love a treason
  Unto my Valentine.

How shall my wan lippes utter
  Their summons to the dedde, —
Where nowe repeate the promise swete,
  So farre my love hath fledd?
My onely love! What musicke fleet
  Shall crosse the walle that barres?
To earthe the burthen mutter,
  Or singe it to the starrs?

Perchance she dwelles a spirite
  In beautye undestroyed

Where brightest starrs are closely sett
  Farre out beyonde the voyd;
If Margaret be risen yet
  Her looke will hither turne,
I knowe that she will heare it,
  And all my trewe heart learne.

But if no resurrection
  Unseale her dwellinge low,
If one so fayre must bide her there
  Until the trumpe shall blowe,
Nathlesse shall Love outvie Despaire,
  (Whilst constant heart is myne)
And, robbed of her perfection,
  Be faithfull to her shrine.

At this blythe season bending
  Ile whisper to the clodde,
To the chill grasse where shadowes passe
  And leaflesse branches nodde;
There keepe my watche, and crye — Alas
  That Love may not forget,
That Joye must have swifte ending
  And Life be laggard yet!

1882

GUESTS AT YULE

Noël! Noël!
Thus sounds each Christmas bell
Across the winter snow.
But what are the little footprints all
That mark the path from the church-yard wall?
They are those of the children waked to-night
From sleep by the Christmas bells and light:
Ring sweetly, chimes! Soft, soft, my rhymes!
Their beds are under the snow.

Noël! Noël!
Carols each Christmas bell.
What are the wraiths of mist
That gather anear the window-pane
Where the winter frost all day has lain?
They are soulless elves, who fain would peer
Within, and laugh at our Christmas cheer:
Ring fleetly, chimes! Swift, swift, my rhymes!
They are made of the mocking mist.

Noël! Noël!
Cease, cease, each Christmas bell!
Under the holly bough,
Where the happy children throng and shout,
What shadow seems to flit about?
Is it the mother, then, who died
Ere the greens were sere last Christmas-tide?
Hush, falling chimes! Cease, cease, my rhymes!
The guests are gathered now.

1882

THE OLD PICTURE-DEALER

THE second landing-place. Above,
  Sun-pictures for a shilling each.
Below, a haunt that Teutons love, —
  Beer, smoke and pretzels all in reach.
Between the two, a mouldy nook
  Where loungers hunt for things of worth —
Engraving, curio, or book —
  Here drifted from all over Earth.

Be the day's traffic more or less,
  Old Brian seeks his Leyden chair
Placed in the ante-room's recess,
  Our connoisseur's securest lair:
Here, turning full the burner's rays,
  Holds long his treasure-trove in sight, —
Upon a painting sets his gaze
  Like some devoted eremite.

The book-worms rummage as they will,
  Loud roars the wonted Broadway din,

Life runs its hackneyed round, — but still
   One tireless boon can Brian win, —
Can picture in this modern time
   A life no more the world shall know,
And dream of Beauty at her prime
   In Parma, with Correggio.

Withered the dealer's face, and old,
   But wearing yet the first surprise
Of him whose eyes the light behold
   Of Italy and Paradise:
Forever blest, forever young,
   The rapt Madonna poises there,
Her praise by hovering cherubs sung,
   Her robes by ether buoyed, not air.

See from the graybeard's meerschaum float
   A cloud of incense! Day or night,
He needs must steal apart to note
   Her grace, her consecrating light.
With less ecstatic worship lay,
   Before his marble goddess prone,
The crippled poet, that last day
   When in the Louvre he made his moan.

Warm grows the radiant masterpiece,
  The sweetness of Correggio!
The visionary hues increase,
  Angelic lustres come and go;
And still, as still in Parma too, —
  In Rome, Bologna, Florence, all, —
Goes on the outer world's ado,
  Life's transitory, harsh recall.

A real Correggio? And here!
  Yes, to the one impassioned heart,
Transfiguring all, the strokes appear
  That mark the perfect master's art.
You question of the proof? You owe
  More faith to fact than fancy? Hush!
Look with expectant eyes, and know,
  With him, the hand that held the brush!

The same wild thought that warmed from stone
  The Venus of the monkish Gest,
The image of Pygmalion,
  Here finds Correggio confest.
And Art requires its votary:
  The Queen of Heaven herself may pine
When these quaint rooms no longer see
  The one that knew her all divine.

Ah, me! ah me, for centuries veiled!
  (The desolate Virgin then may say,)
Once more my rainbow tints are paled
  With that unquestioning soul away —
Whose faith compelled the sun, the stars,
  To yield their halos for my sake,
And saw through Time's obscuring bars
  The Parmese master's glory break!

1883

THE WORLD WELL LOST

THAT year? Yes, doubtless I remember still, —
Though why take count of every wind that blows!
'T was plain, men said, that Fortune used me ill
That year, — the self-same year I met with Rose.

Crops failed; wealth took a flight; house, treasure, land,
Slipped from my hold — thus plenty comes and goes.
One friend I had, but he too loosed his hand
(Or was it I?) the year I met with Rose.

There was a war, I think; some rumor, too,
Of famine, pestilence, fire, deluge, snows;
Things went awry. My rivals, straight in view,
Throve, spite of all; but I, — I met with Rose.

That year my white-faced Alma pined and died:
  Some trouble vexed her quiet heart, — who
      knows?
Not I, who scarcely missed her from my side,
  Or aught else gone, the year I met with Rose.

Was there no more? Yes, that year life began:
  All life before a dream, false joys, light woes, —
All after-life compressed within the span
  Of that one year, — the year I met with Rose!

1883

HEBE

SEE, what a beauty! Half-shut eyes, —
  Hide all buff, and without a break
To the tail's brown tuft that mostly lies
  So quiet one thinks her scarce awake;
But pass too near, one step too free,
  You find her slumber a devil's truce:
Up comes that paw, — all plush, you see, —
  Out four claws, fit for Satan's use.

'Ware! Just a sleeve's breadth closer then,
  And your last appearance on any stage!
Loll, if you like, by Daniel's Den,
  But clear and away from Hebe's cage: —
That 's Hebe! listen to that purr,
  Rumbling as from the ground below:
Strange, when the ring begins to stir,
  The fleshings always vex her so.

You think 't were a rougher task by far
  To tame her mate with the sooty mane?

A splendid bronze for a showman's car,
  And listless enough for bit and rein.
But Hebe is — just like all her sex —
  Not good, then bad, — be sure of that:
In either case 't would a sage perplex
  To make them out, both woman and cat.

A curious record, Hebe's. Reared
  In Italy; age, — that 's hard to fix;
Trained from a cub, until she feared
  The lash, and learned her round of tricks;
Always a traveller, — one of two
  A woman-tamer took in hand,
Whipped them, coaxed them, — and so they grew
  To fawn or cower at her command.

None but Florina — that was her name
  And this the story of Hebe here —
Entered their cage; the brutes were tame
  As kittens, though, their mistress near.
A tall, proud wench as ever was seen,
  Supple and handsome, full of grace:
The world would bow to a real queen
  That had Florina's form and face.

Her lover — for one she had, of course —
 Was Marco, acrobat, circus-star,
The lightest foot on a running horse,
 The surest leap from a swinging bar;
And she, — so jealous he dared not touch
 A woman's hand, and, truth to say,
He had no humor to tease her much
 Till a girl in spangles crossed their way.

'T was at Marseilles, the final scene:
 This pretty rider joined the ring,
Ma'am'selle Celeste or Victorine,
 And captured him under Florina's wing.
They hid their meetings, but when, you see,
 Doubt holds the candle, love will show,
And in love's division the one of three,
 Whose share is lessened, needs must know.

One night, then, after the throng outpoured
 From the show, and the lions my Lady's power
Had been made to feel, with lash that scored
 And eye that cowed them, a snarling hour; —
(They were just in the mood for pleasantry
 Of those holidays when saints were thrown

To beasts, and the Romans, entrance-free,
Clapped hands;) — that night, as she stood alone,

Florina, Queen of the Lions, called
Sir Marco toward her, while her hand
Still touched the spring of a door that walled
Her subjects safe within Lion-land.
He came there panting, hot from the ring,
So brave a figure that one might know
Among all his tribe he must be king, —
If in some wild tract you met him so.

"Do you love me still," she asked, "as when
You swore it first?" "Have never a doubt!"
"But I have a fancy — men are men,
And one whim drives another out," —
"What fancy? Is this all? Have done:
You tire me." "Look you, Marco! oh,
I should die if another woman won
Your love, — but would kill you first, you know!"

"Kill me? and how, — with a jealous tongue?"
"Thus!" quoth Florina, and slipped the bolt

Of the cage's door, and headlong flung
  Sir Marco, ere he could breathe, the dolt!
Plump on the lion he bounced, and fell
  Beyond, and Hebe leapt for him there,—
No need for their lady's voice to tell
  The work in hand for that ready pair.

They say one would n't have cared to see
  The group commingled, man and beast,
Or to hear the shrieks and roars,—all three
  One red, the feasters and the feast!
Guns, pistols, blazed, till the lion sprawled,
  Shot dead, but Hebe held to her prey
And drank his blood, while keepers bawled
  And their hot irons made yon scars that day.

But the woman? True, I had forgot:
  She never flinched at the havoc made,
Nor gave one cry, but there on the spot
  Drove to the heart her poniard-blade,
Straight, like a man, and fell, nor stirred
  Again;—so that fine pair were dead;
One lied, and the other kept her word,—
  And death pays debts, when all is said.

HEBE

So they hustled Hebe out of France,
  To Spain, or may be to England first.
Then hitherward over seas, by chance,
  She came as you see her, always athirst,—
As if, like the tigresses that slink
  In the village canes of Hindostan,
Of one rare draught she loves to think,
  And ever to get it must plan and plan.

1884

SOUVENIR DE JEUNESSE

When Sibyl kept her tryst with me, the harvest
 moon was rounded,
In evening hush through pathways lush with
 fern we reached the glade;
The rippling river soft and low with fairy plashes
 sounded,
The silver poplar rustled as we sat within its
 shade.

"And why," she whispered, "evermore should
 lovers meet to sunder?
Where stars arise in other skies let other lips
 than mine
Their sorrows lisp, and other hearts at love's delay-
 ing wonder —
O stay!"— and soon her tearful eyes were each
 a pearly shrine.

I soothed her fears and stayed her tears, her hands
 in mine enfolding,

And then we cared no more for aught save this one hour we had;
Upwelled that dreamful selfish tide of young Love's rapture, holding
The fair round world itself in pledge to make us still more glad.

For us the night was musical, for us the meadows shining;
The summer air was odorous that we might breathe and love;
Sweet Nature throbbed for us alone — her mother-soul divining
No fonder pair that fleeting hour her zephyrs sighed above.

Amid the nodding rushes the heron drank his tipple,
The night-hawk's cry and whir anigh a deeper stillness made,
A thousand little starlights danced upon the river's ripple,
And the silver poplar rustled as we kissed within its shade.

1884

A VIGIL

I WALK the lane's dim hollow, —
    Past is the twilight hour,
But stealthy shadows follow
    And Night withholds her power,
For somewhere in the eastern sky
    The shrouded moon is high.

Dews from the wild rose drip unheard, —
    Their unforgotten scent
With that of woods and grasses blent;
    No muffled flight of bird,
No whispering voice, my footfall stops;
No breeze amid the poplar-tops
    The smallest leaf has stirred.

Yet round me, here and there,
    A little fluttering wind
Plays now, — these senses have divined
    A breath across my hair, —
A touch, — that on my forehead lies,

And presses long
These lips so mute of song,
And now, with kisses cool, my half-shut eyes.

This night? O what is here!
What viewless aura clings
So fitfully, so near,
On this returning eventide
When Memory will not be denied
Unfettered wings?

My arms reach out, — in vain, —
They fold the air:
And yet — that wandering breath again!
Too vague to make her phantom plain,
Too tender for despair.

1884

THE STAR BEARER

THERE were seven angels erst that spanned
Heaven's roadway out through space,
Lighting with stars, by God's command,
The fringe of that high place
Whence plumèd beings in their joy,
The servitors His thoughts employ,
Fly ceaselessly. No goodlier band
Looked upward to His face.

There, on bright hovering wings that tire
Never, they rested mute,
Nor of far journeys had desire,
Nor of the deathless fruit;
For in and through each angel soul
All waves of life and knowledge roll,
Even as to nadir streamed the fire
Of their torches resolute.

They lighted Michael's outpost through
Where fly the armored brood,

And the wintry Earth their omens knew
Of Spring's beatitude;
Rude folk, ere yet the promise came,
Gave to their orbs a heathen name,
Saying how steadfast in men's view
The watchful Pleiads stood.

All in the solstice of the year,
When the sun apace must turn,
The seven bright angels 'gan to hear
Heaven's twin gates outward yearn:
Forth with its light and minstrelsy
A lordly troop came speeding by,
And joyed to see each cresset sphere
So gloriously burn.

Staying his fearless passage then
The Captain of that host
Spake with strong voice: "We bear to men
God's gift the uttermost,
Whereof the oracle and sign
Sibyl and sages may divine:
A star shall blazon in their ken,
Borne with us from your post.

"This night the Heir of Heaven's throne
A new-born mortal lies!
Since Earth's first morning hath not shone
Such joy in seraph eyes."
He spake. The least in honor there
Answered with longing like a prayer, —
"My star, albeit thenceforth unknown,
Shall light for you Earth's skies."

Onward the blessed legion swept,
That angel at the head;
(Where seven of old their station kept
There are six that shine instead.)
Straight hitherward came troop and star;
Like some celestial bird afar
Into Earth's night the cohort leapt
With beauteous wings outspread.

Dazzling the East beneath it there,
The Star gave out its rays:
Right through the still Judean air
The shepherds see it blaze, —
They see the plume-borne heavenly throng,
And hear a burst of that high song
Of which in Paradise aware
Saints count their years but days.

For they sang such music as, I deem,
In God's chief court of joys,
Had stayed the flow of the crystal stream
And made souls in mid-flight poise;
They sang of Glory to Him most High,
Of Peace on Earth abidingly,
And of all delights the which, men dream,
Nor sin nor grief alloys.

Breathless the kneeling shepherds heard,
Charmed from their first rude fear,
Nor while that music dwelt had stirred
Were it a month or year:
And Mary Mother drank its flow,
Couched with her Babe divine, — and, lo!
Ere falls the last ecstatic word
Three Holy Kings draw near.

Whenas the star-led shining train
Wheeled from their task complete,
Skyward from over Bethlehem's plain
They sped with rapture fleet;
And the angel of that orient star,
Thenceforth where Heaven's lordliest are,
Stands with a harp, while Christ doth reign,
A seraph near His feet.

1887

EVENTIDE

THE sunset fires old Portsmouth spires,
  Out creeps the ebbing tide;
Beyond the battery-point I see
  A glimmering schooner glide;
White flares the turning Whale-back light,
  The silent ground-swell rolls;
Low and afar shines one red star
  Above the Isles of Shoals.

1888

HELEN KELLER

Mute, sightless visitant,
From what uncharted world
Hast voyaged into Life's rude sea,
With guidance scant;
As if some bark mysteriously
Should hither glide, with spars aslant
And sails all furled?

In what perpetual dawn,
Child of the spotless brow,
Hast kept thy spirit far withdrawn —
Thy birthright undefiled?
What views to thy sealed eyes appear?
What voices mayst thou hear
Speak as we know not how?
Of grief and sin hast thou,
O radiant child,
Even thou, a share? Can mortal taint
Have power on thee unfearing
The woes our sight, our hearing,
Learn from Earth's crime and plaint?

Not as we see
Earth, sky, insensate forms, ourselves,
Thou seest, — but vision-free
Thy fancy soars and delves,
Albeit no sounds to us relate
The wondrous things
Thy brave imaginings
Within their starry night create.

Pity thy unconfined
Clear spirit, whose enfranchised eyes
Use not their grosser sense?
Ah, no! thy bright intelligence
Hath its own Paradise,
A realm wherein to hear and see
Things hidden from our kind.
Not thou, not thou — 't is we
Are deaf, are dumb, are blind!

1888

PORTRAIT D'UNE DAME ESPAGNOLE

(FORTUNY)

THE hand that drew thee lies in Roman soil,
Whilst on the canvas thou hast deathless grown,
Endued by him who deemed it meaner toil
To give the world a portrait save thine own.

Yet had he found thy peer, and Rome forborne
Such envy of his conquest over Time,
Beauty had waked, and Art another morn
Had gained, and ceased to sorrow for her prime.

What spirit was it — where the masters are —
Brooding the gloom and glory that were Spain,
Through centuries waited in its orb afar
Until our age Fortuny's brush should gain?

What stroke but his who pictured in their state
Queen, beggar, noble, Philip's princely brood,

Could thus the boast of Seville recreate,
  Even when one like thee before him stood?

Like thee, own child of Spain, whose beauteous pride,
  Desire, disdain, all sins thy mien express,
Should need no absolution — hadst thou died
  Unhouselled, in their imaged loveliness.

All this had Fate decreed, — the antique skill,
  The halt, the poise, the long auspicious day, —
Yielding this once, thy triumph to fulfil,
  Velasquez' sceptre to Fortuny's sway.

Shine from thy cloud of night, fair star, nor fear
  Oblivion, though men thy dust inurn,
For who may bid thy counterpart appear
  Until the hand that drew thee shall return!

1889

A SEA-CHANGE, AT KELP ROCK

JUST at this full noon of summer
   There 's a touch, unfelt before,
Charms our Coastland, smoothing from her
   The last crease her forehead wore:
She, too, drains the sun-god's potion,
   Quits her part of anchorite,
Smiles to see her leaden ocean
   Sparkle in the austral light;

While the tidal depths beneath her
   Palpitate with warmth and love,
And the infinite pure æther
   Floods the yearning creek and cove,
Harbor, woodland, promontory,
   Swarded fields that slope between,—
And our gray tower, tinged with glory,
   Midway flames above the scene.

On this day of all most luring,
   This one morn of all the year,

A SEA-CHANGE, AT KELP ROCK

Read I — soul and body curing
   In the seaward loggia here —
Once, twice, thrice, that chorus sweetest
   (Fortune's darling, Sophokles!)
Of the grove whose steeds are fleetest,
   Nurtured by the sacred breeze;

Of Kolonos, where in clusters
   Blooms narcissus — where unfold
Ivied trees their leafy lustres
   And the crocus spreads its gold;
Where the nightingales keep singing
   And the streamlets never cease,
To the son of Laius bringing
   Rest at last, forgiveness, peace.

Drops the book — but from its prison
   Tell me now what antique spell,
Through the unclaspt cover risen,
   Moves the waves I know so well;
Bids me find in them hereafter,
   Dimpled to their utmost zone
With the old innumerous laughter,
   An Ægean of my own?

A SEA-CHANGE, AT KELP ROCK

Even so: the blue Ægean
  Through our tendriled arches smiles,
And the distant empyrean
  Curves to kiss enchanted isles:
Isles of Shoals, I know — yet fancy
  This one day shall have free range,
And yon isles her necromancy
  Shall to those of Hellas change.

Look! beyond the lanterned pharos
  Girt with reefs that evermore,
Lashed and foaming, cry "Beware us!"
  Cloud-white sails draw nigh the shore:
Sails, methinks, of burnished galleys
  Wafting dark-browed maids within,
From those island hills and valleys,
  Dread Athene's grace to win.

Sandalled, coiffed, and white-robed maidens,
  Chanting in their carven boats;
List! and hear anon the cadence
  Of their virginal fresh notes.
You shall hear the choric hymnos,
  Or some clear prosodion
Known to Delos, Naxos, Lemnos,
  Isles beneath the eastern sun.

'T is the famed Æolian quire
   Bearing Pallas flowers and fruit —
Some with white hands touch the lyre,
   Some with red lips kiss the flute;
You shall see the vestured priestess,
   Violet-crowned, her chalice swing,
Ere yon cerylus has ceased his
   Swirl upon "the sea-blue wing."

In the great Panathenæa
   Climbing marble porch and stair,
Soon before the statued Dea
   Votive baskets they shall bear,
Sacred palm, and fragrant censer,
   Wine-cups —
                  But what vapor hoar,
What cloud-curtain dense, and denser,
   Looms between them and the shore?

Off, thou Norseland Terror, clouding
   Hellas with the jealous wraith
Which, the gods of old enshrouding,
   Froze their hearts, the poet saith!

Vain the cry: from yon abysm
  Now the fog-horn's woeful blast—
Stern New England's exorcism!—
  Ends my vision of the past.

1890

HAREBELL

A REPARATION

"Grant him," I said, "a well-earned name,
The stage's knight, the keen assayer
Of parts whence all save greatness came,
But — not a player.

"Strange, as of fate's perverseness, this
Proud, eager soul, this fine-strung creature
Should seem forever just to miss
That touch of nature;

"The instinct she so lightly gives
Some fellow at his rivals snarling,
Some churl who gains the boards, and lives
Transformed — her darling!"

"You think so?" he replied. "Well, I
Thought likewise, maugre Lanciotto,

And Yorick, though his Cassius nigh
    Won Hamlet's motto.

"But would you learn, as I, his clew
  To nature's heart, and judge him fairly —
Go see his rustic bard, go view
    His Man o' Airlie.

"See that defenceless minstrel brought
  From hope to wan despair, from laughter
To frenzy's moan: the image wrought
    Will haunt you after.

"Then see him crowned at last! If such
  A guerdon waits the stricken poet,
'T were well, you 'll own, to bear as much —
    Even die, to know it."

"Bravo!" cried I, "I too, the thrill
  Must feel which thus your blood can waken."
And once I saw upon the bill
    That part retaken;

But leagues of travel stretched between
  Me and that idyl played so rarely:
And then — his death! nor had I seen
    "The Man o' Airlie."

My failure; not the actor's, loved
  By all to art and nature loyal;
Not his, whom Harebell's passion proved
    Of the blood royal.

1891

THE PILGRIMS

O PILGRIM from the Indies!
 O guest from out the North,
Where low and dun the midnight sun
 Upon the wave rides forth!
What country is most dear of all
 Beneath the heaven blue?
The dearest land is one's own land,
 Go search the wide world through.

O know you not that henceforth
 All countries are as one?
Ere summer fail, the world shall hail
 Its golden year begun.
But still each pilgrim answering names
 The clime that gave him birth:
One's own land is the dearest land
 Of all fair lands on earth.

Children's Song,
Columbian Exposition, 1893

MORS BENEFICA

GIVE me to die unwitting of the day,
 And stricken in Life's brave heat, with senses clear:
 Not swathed and couched until the lines appear
Of Death's wan mask upon this withering clay,
But as that old man eloquent made way
 From Earth, a nation's conclave hushed anear;
 Or as the chief whose fates, that he may hear
The victory, one glorious moment stay.
Or, if not thus, then with no cry in vain,
 No ministrant beside to ward and weep,
Hand upon helm I would my quittance gain
 In some wild turmoil of the waters deep,
 And sink content into a dreamless sleep
(Spared grave and shroud) below the ancient main.

1893

PROEM TO A VICTORIAN ANTHOLOGY

ENGLAND! since Shakespeare died no loftier day
For thee than lights herewith a century's goal, —
Nor statelier exit of heroic soul
Conjoined with soul heroic, — nor a lay
Excelling theirs who made renowned thy sway
Even as they heard the billows which outroll
Thine ancient sea, and left their joy and dole
In song, and on the strand their mantles gray.
Star-rayed with fame thine Abbey windows loom
Above his dust, whom the Venetian barge
Bore to the main; who passed the twofold marge
To slumber in thy keeping, — yet make room
For the great Laurifer, whose chanting large
And sweet shall last until our tongue's far doom.

1895

ON WHITE CARNATIONS GIVEN ME FOR MY BIRTHDAY

Exquisite tufts of perfume and of light,
  Fair gift of Summer unto Autumn borne,
Were but the years ye calendar as white,
  As sweet, as you, Age could not be forlorn.

Yet, beauteous symbols of my only gain —
  Love, portioned from your givers' envied share,
Honor, whose laurel at their feet hath lain —
  Make me this night of Life's waste unaware!

October 8, 1894

FATHER JARDINE

TRINITY CHURCH, ST. LOUIS

AROUND his loins, when the last breath had gone
From the gaunt frame — and death's encroaching mist,
A veil betwixt earth left and heaven won,
Told naught of all it wist —

Close to the flesh, sore-lashed by waves of pain,
They found the iron girth that ate his side,
Its links worn bright : the cruel, secret chain,
They found it when he died.

Son of the Church, though worldlings spake her creed
And smiled askance, even in the altar fold,
This man, this piteous soul, believed indeed
With the stern faith of old.

FATHER JARDINE

Unquestioning aught, aye, in the eager West
  Surcharged with life that mocks the vague unknown,
His ligature of anguish unconfest
    He wore alone — alone.

Alone? but trebly welded links of fate
  More lives than one are bidden to endure,
Forged in a chain's indissoluble weight
    Of agonies more sure.

His torture was self-torture; to his soul
  No jest of time irrevocably brought
A woe more grim than underneath the stole
    His gnawing cincture wrought.

Belike my garments, — yes, or thine, — conceal
  The sorer wound, the pitiabler throe,
Not even the traitor Death shall quite reveal
    For his rough mutes to know.

What the heart hungered for and was denied,
  Still foiled with guerdons for a world to see

And envy it, — this furrows deep and wide
Its grooves in thee — in me.

Borne, always borne — what martyrdoms assoil
The laden soul from hostile chance and blind?
Nor time can loose the adamantine coil,
Nor Azrael unbind.

Redemption for the priest! but naught their gain
Who forfeit still the one thing asked of Earth,
Knowing all penance light beside this pain —
All pleasure, nothing worth.

1894

FIN DE SIÈCLE

Now making exit to the outer vast
  Our century speeds, and shall retain no more
Its perihelion splendor, save to cast
  A search-light on the chartless course before.

I hear the murmur of our kind, whose eyes
  Follow the spread of that phantasmal ray;
Who see as infants see, nor can surmise
  Aright of what is near — what far away.

I hear the jest, the threnody, the low
  Recount of dreams which down the years have
      fled, —
Of fair romance now shattered with love's bow,
  Of legend brought to test, and passion dead.

Dark Science broods in Fancy's hermitage,
  The rainbow fades, — and hushed, they say, is
      Song

With those high bards who lingering charmed the age
Ere one by one they joined the statued throng.

I hear the dirge for beauty sped, and faith
Astray in space and time's far archways lost,
Till Life itself becomes a tenuous wraith,
A wandering shade whom wandering shades accost.

Their light sad plaint I hear who thus divine
The future, counselling that all is done, —
Naught left for art's sweet touch — but to refine,
For courage — but to face the setting sun.

I hear, yet have no will to falter so.
We seek out matter's alchemy, and tame
Force to our needs, but what shall make us know
Whether the twain are parted, or the same?

The same! then conscious substance, fetterless
The more when most subdued to Will's control,

Free though in bonds, foredestined to progress, —
  Ever, and ever still — the soul, the soul:

The unvexed spirit, to whose sure intent
  All else is relative. Or large or small,
The Afrit, cloud or being, free or pent,
  Enshrouds, impenetrates, and masters all.

No grain of sand too narrow to enfold
  The spirit's incarnation; no vast land
And sea, but, readjusted to their mould,
  It deems Atlantis scarce a grain of sand.

Time's intervals are ages; planets sleep
  In death, or blaze in living light afar;
Thought answers thought; deep calleth unto deep
  Alike within the globule and the star.

Ay, even the rock-bound globe, which still doth feign
  Itself inanimate, itself shall seem
From yonder void a bead upon the train
  Of heaven's warder rayed with beam on beam.

Life, when the harper tunes his shrillest string,
   As to low thunder lends a finer ear
Unseen. Niagara's slow vibrating
   Is but the treble of the greater sphere,

Whose lightest orchestras such movements play
   As mock the forest's moan, the bass profound
Of surges that against deep barriers stay
   Their might, in throes which shake the ancient
         ground.

Will, consciousness, the tenant lord of all,
   Self-tenanted, is still the wrinkled wave
Which climbs a wave upon the clambering wall
   Beyond, or in the hollow seeks a grave.

We time the ray, we pulsate with the fling
   Of ether — feel the sure magnetic thrill
Make answer to each sombre vortex ring
   Whirled with the whirling sun that binds us
         still;

That binds us, bound itself from girth to pole
   By some unconquerable deathless force

Akin to this which thinks, acts, feels, — the soul
Of man, forever eddying like its source.

Passion and jest, the laugh and wail of earth,
High thought and speech, the rare considerings
Of beauty that to fairer art gives birth,
The winnowing of poesy's swift wings, —

These — though the hoary century inurn
Our great — no gathering mould of time shall
clod:
They bide their hour, they pass but to return
With men, as now, the progeny of God.

1892

II

OTHER SONGS AND BALLADS

FALSTAFF'S SONG

WHERE 's he that died o' Wednesday?
  What place on earth hath he?
A tailor's yard beneath, I wot,
  Where worms approaching be;
For the wight that died o' Wednesday,
  Just laid the light below,
Is dead as the varlet turned to clay
  A score of years ago.

Where 's he that died o' Sabba' day?
  Good Lord, I 'd not be he!
The best of days is foul enough
  From this world's fare to flee;
And the saint that died o' Sabba' day,
  With his grave turf yet to grow,
Is dead as the sinner brought to pray
  A hundred years ago.

Where 's he that died o' yesterday?
  What better chance hath he

FALSTAFF'S SONG

To clink the can and toss the pot
  When this night's junkets be?
For the lad that died o' yesterday
  Is just as dead — ho! ho! —
As the whoreson knave men laid away
  A thousand years ago.

PROVENÇAL LOVERS

AUCASSIN AND NICOLETTE

WITHIN the garden of Beaucaire
He met her by a secret stair,—
The night was centuries ago.
Said Aucassin, "My love, my pet,
These old confessors vex me so!
They threaten all the pains of hell
Unless I give you up, ma belle;"—
Said Aucassin to Nicolette.

"Now, who should there in Heaven be
To fill your place, ma très-douce mie?
To reach that spot I little care!
There all the droning priests are met;
All the old cripples, too, are there
That unto shrines and altars cling
To filch the Peter-pence we bring;"—
Said Aucassin to Nicolette.

"There are the barefoot monks and friars
With gowns well tattered by the briars,
The saints who lift their eyes and whine:
I like them not — a starveling set!
Who'd care with folk like these to dine?
The other road 't were just as well
That you and I should take, ma belle!" —
Said Aucassin to Nicolette.

"To purgatory I would go
With pleasant comrades whom we know,
Fair scholars, minstrels, lusty knights
Whose deeds the land will not forget,
The captains of a hundred fights,
The men of valor and degree:
We'll join that gallant company," —
Said Aucassin to Nicolette.

"There, too, are jousts and joyance rare,
And beauteous ladies debonair,
The pretty dames, the merry brides,
Who with their wedded lords coquette
And have a friend or two besides, —
And all in gold and trappings gay,
With furs, and crests in vair and gray;" —
Said Aucassin to Nicolette.

"Sweet players on the cithern strings,
And they who roam the world like kings,
Are gathered there, so blithe and free!
Pardie! I'd join them now, my pet,
If you went also, ma douce mie!
The joys of heaven I'd forego
To have you with me there below,"—
Said Aucassin to Nicolette.

1878

THE WEDDING-DAY

I

Sweetheart, name the day for me
When we two shall wedded be.
Make it ere another moon,
While the meadows are in tune,
And the trees are blossoming,
And the robins mate and sing.
Whisper, love, and name a day
In this merry month of May.

No, no, no,
You shall not escape me so!
Love will not forever wait;
Roses fade when gathered late.

II

Fie, for shame, Sir Malcontent!
How can time be better spent

Than in wooing? I would wed
When the clover blossoms red,
When the air is full of bliss,
And the sunshine like a kiss.
If you 're good I 'll grant a boon:
You shall have me, sir, in June.

Nay, nay, nay,
Girls for once should have their way!
If you love me, wait till June:
Rosebuds wither, picked too soon.

1878

THE DUTCH PATROL

WHEN Christmas-Eve is ended,
  Just at the noon of night,
Rare things are seen by mortal een
  That have the second sight.
In St. Mark's church-yard then
  They see the shape arise
Of him who ruled Nieuw Amsterdam
  And here in slumber lies.

His face, beneath the close black cap,
  Has a martial look and grim;
On either side his locks fall wide
  To the broad collar's rim;
His sleeves are slashed; the velvet coat
  Is fashioned Hollandese
Above his fustian breeches, trimmed
  With scarf-knots at the knees.

His leg of flesh is hosed in silk;
  His wooden leg is bound,

As well befits a conqueror's,
With silver bands around.
He reads the lines that mark
His tablet on the wall,
Where boldly PETRUS STUYVESANT
Stands out beyond them all.

"'T is well!" he says, and sternly smiles,
"They hold our memory dear;
Nor rust nor moss hath crept across;
'T will last this many a year."
Then down the path he strides,
And through the iron gate,
Where the sage Nine Men, his councillors,
Their Governor await.

Here are Van der Donck and Van Cortlandt,
A triplet more of Vans,
And Hendrick Kip of the haughty lip,
And Govert Loockermans,
Jan Jansen Dam, and Jansen,
Of whom our annals tell, —
All risen this night their lord to greet
At sound of the Christmas bell.

THE DUTCH PATROL

Nine lusty forms in linsey coats,
  Puffed sleeves and ample hose!
Each burgher smokes a Flemish pipe
  To warm his ancient nose;
The smoke-wreaths rise like mist,
  The smokers all are mute,
Yet all, with pipes thrice waving slow,
  Brave Stuyvesant salute.

Then into ranks they fall,
  And step out three by three,
And he of the wooden leg and staff
  In front walks solemnly.
Along their wonted course
  The phantom troop patrol,
To see how fares Nieuw Amsterdam,
  And what the years unroll.

Street after street and mile on mile,
  From river bound to bound,
From old St. Mark's to Whitehall Point,
  They foot the limits round;
From Maiden Lane to Corlaer's Hook
  The Dutchmen's pypen glow,
But never a word from their lips is heard,
  And none their passing know.

Ere the first streak of dawn
St. Mark's again they near,
And by a vault the Nine Men halt,
Their Governor's voice to hear.
"Mynheeren," he says, "ye see
Each year our borders spread!
Lo, one by one, the landmarks gone,
And marvels come instead!

"Not even a windmill left,
Nor a garden-plot we knew,
And but a paling marks the spot
Where erst my pear-tree grew.
Our walks are wearier still, —
Perchance and it were best,
So little of worth is left on earth,
To break no more our rest?"

Thus speaks old Petrus doubtfully
And shakes his valiant head,
When — on the roofs a sound of hoofs,
A rattling, pattering tread!
The bells of reindeer tinkle,
The Dutchmen plainly spy
St. Nicholas, who drives his team
Across the roof-tops nigh.

"Beshrew me for a craven!"
  Cries Petrus — "All goes well!
Our patron saint still makes his round
  At sound of the Christmas bell.
So long as stanch St. Nicholas
  Shall guard these houses tall,
There shall come no harm from hostile arm —
  No evil chance befall!

"The yongens and the meisjes
  Shall have their hosen filled;
The butcher and the baker,
  And every honest guild,
Shall merrily thrive and flourish;
  Good-night, and be of cheer;
We may safely lay us down again
  To sleep another year!"

Once more the pipes are waved,
  Stout Petrus gives the sign,
The misty smoke enfolds them round, —
  Him and his burghers nine.
All, when the cloud has lifted,
  Have vanished quite away,
And the crowing cock and steeple clock
  Proclaim 't is Christmas-Day.

1882

WITCHCRAFT

I

A. D. 1692

Soe, Mistress Anne, faire neighbour myne,
  How rides a witche when nighte-winds blowe?
Folk saye that you are none too goode
To joyne the crewe in Salem woode,
When one you wot of gives the signe:
  Righte well, methinks, the pathe you knowe.

In Meetinge-time I watched you well,
  Whiles godly Master Parris prayed:
Your folded hands laye on your booke;
But Richard answered to a looke
That fain would tempt him unto hell,
  Where, Mistress Anne, your place is made.

You looke into my Richard's eyes
  With evill glances shamelesse growne;
I found about his wriste a hair,
And guesse what fingers tyed it there:

He shall not lightly be your prize—
  Your Master firste shall take his owne.

'T is not in nature he should be
  (Who loved me soe when Springe was greene)
A childe, to hange upon your gowne!
He loved me well in Salem Towne
Until this wanton witcherie
  His hearte and myne crept dark betweene.

Last Sabbath nighte, the gossips saye,
  Your goodman missed you from his side.
He had no strength to move, untill
Agen, as if in slumber still,
Beside him at the dawne you laye.
  Tell, nowe, what meanwhile did betide.

Dame Anne, mye hate goe with you fleete
  As driftes the Bay fogg overhead—
Or over yonder hill-topp, where
There is a tree ripe fruite shall bear
When, neighbour myne, your wicked feet
  The stones of Gallowes Hill shall tread.

II

A. D. 1884

Our great-great-grandpapas had schooled
  Your fancies, Lita, were you born
In days when Cotton Mather ruled
  And damask petticoats were worn!
Your pretty ways, your mocking air,
  Had passed, mayhap, for Satan's wiles —
As fraught with danger, then and there,
  To you, as now to us your smiles.

Why not? Were inquest to begin,
  The tokens are not far to seek:
Item — the dimple of your chin;
  Item — that freckle on your cheek.
Grace shield his simple soul from harm
  Who enters yon flirtation niche,
Or trusts in whispered counter-charm,
  Alone with such a parlous witch!

Your fan a wand is, in disguise;
  It conjures, and we straight are drawn
Within a witches' Paradise
  Of music, germans, roses, lawn.

So through the season, where you go,
  All else than Lita men forget:
One needs no second-sight to know
  That sorcery is rampant yet.

Now, since the bars no more await
  Fair maids that practise sable arts,
Take heed, while I pronounce the fate
  Of her who thus ensnares men's hearts:
In time you shall a wizard meet
  With spells more potent than your own,
And you shall know your master, Sweet,
  And for these witcheries atone.

For you at his behest shall wear
  A veil, and seek with him the church,
And at the altar rail forswear
  The craft that left you in the lurch;
But oft thereafter, musing long,
  With smile, and sigh, and conscience-twitch,
You shall too late confess the wrong —
  A captive and repentant witch.

1884

AARON BURR'S WOOING

FROM the commandant's quarters on Westchester height
The blue hills of Ramapo lie in full sight;
On their slope gleam the gables that shield his heart's queen,
But the redcoats are wary — the Hudson 's between.
Through the camp runs a jest: "There 's no moon — 't will be dark;
'T is odds little Aaron will go on a spark!"
And the toast of the troopers is: "Pickets, lie low,
And good luck to the colonel and Widow Prevost!"

Eight miles to the river he gallops his steed,
Lays him bound in the barge, bids his escort make speed,
Loose their swords, sit athwart, through the fleet reach yon shore.
Not a word — not a plash of the thick-muffled oar!

Once across, once again in the seat and away —
Five leagues are soon over when love has the say;
And "Old Put" and his rider a bridle-path know
To the Hermitage manor of Madame Prevost.

Lightly done! but he halts in the grove's deepest glade,
Ties his horse to a birch, trims his cue, slings his blade,
Wipes the dust and the dew from his smooth, handsome face,
With the 'kerchief she broidered and bordered in lace;
Then slips through the box-rows and taps at the hall,
Sees the glint of a waxlight, a hand white and small,
And the door is unbarred by herself all aglow —
Half in smiles, half in tears — Theodosia Prevost.

Alack for the soldier that's buried and gone!
What's a volley above him, a wreath on his stone,
Compared with sweet life and a wife for one's view
Like this dame, ripe and warm in her India fichu?
She chides her bold lover, yet holds him more dear,
For the daring that brings him a night-rider here;

British gallants by day through her doors come and go,
But a Yankee 's the winner of Theo Prevost.

Where 's the widow or maid with a mouth to be kist,
When Burr comes a-wooing, that long would resist?
Lights and wine on the beaufet, the shutters all fast,
And "Old Put" stamps in vain till an hour has flown past —
But an hour, for eight leagues must be covered ere day;
Laughs Aaron, "Let Washington frown as he may,
When he hears of me next, in a raid on the foe,
He 'll forgive this night's tryst with the Widow Prevost!"

1886

COUSIN LUCRECE

HERE where the curfew
  Still, they say, rings,
Time rested long ago,
  Folding his wings;
Here, on old Norwich's
  Out-along road,
Cousin Lucretia
  Had her abode.

Norridge, not Nor-wich
  (See Mother Goose),
Good enough English
  For a song's use.
Side and roof shingled,
  All of a piece,
Here was the cottage
  Of Cousin Lucrece.

Living forlornly
  On nothing a year,

How she took comfort
  Does not appear;
How kept her body,
  On what they gave,
Out of the poor-house,
  Out of the grave.

Highly connected?
  Straight as the Nile
Down from "the Gard'ners"
  Of Gardiner's Isle;
(Three bugles, chevron gules,
  Hand upon sword),
Great-great-granddaughter
  Of the third lord.

Bent almost double,
  Deaf as a witch,
Gout her chief trouble —
  Just as if rich;
Vain of her ancestry,
  Mouth all agrin,
Nose half-way meeting her
  Sky-pointed chin.

Ducking her forehead-top,
  Wrinkled and bare,
With a colonial
  Furbelowed air
Greeting her next of kin,
  Nephew and niece, —
Foolish old, prating old
  Cousin Lucrece.

Once every year she had
  All she could eat:
Turkey and cranberries,
  Pudding and sweet;
Every Thanksgiving,
  Up to the great
House of her kinsman, was
  Driven in state.

Oh, what a sight to see,
  Rigged in her best!
Wearing the famous gown
  Drawn from her chest, —
Worn, ere King George's reign
  Here chanced to cease,
Once by a forbear
  Of Cousin Lucrece.

Damask brocaded,
Cut very low ;
Short sleeves and finger-mitts
Fit for a show ;
Palsied neck shaking her
Rust-yellow curls,
Rattling its roundabout
String of mock pearls ;

Over her noddle,
Draggled and stark,
Two ostrich feathers —
Brought from the ark.
Shoes of frayed satin,
All heel and toe,
On her poor crippled feet
Hobbled below.

My ! how the Justice's
Sons and their wives
Laughed ; while the little folk
Ran for their lives,
Asking if beldames
Out of the past,
Old fairy godmothers,
Always could last ?

COUSIN LUCRECE

No! One Thanksgiving,
  Bitterly cold,
After they took her home
  (Ever so old),
In her great chair she sank,
  There to find peace;
Died in her ancient dress —
  Poor old Lucrece.

1892

HUNTINGTON HOUSE

LADIES, Ladies Huntington, your father served, we
know,
As aide-de-camp to Washington — you often told
us so;
And when you sat you side by side in that ances-
tral pew,
We knew his ghost sat next the door, and very
proud of you.

Ladies, Ladies Huntington, like you there are no
more:
Nancy, Sarah, Emily, Louise, — proud maidens
four;
Nancy tall and angular, Louise a rosy dear,
And Emily as fine as lace but just a little sere.

What was it, pray, your life within the mansion
grand and old,
Four dormers in its gambrel-roof, their shingles
grim with mould?

How dwelt you in your spinsterhood, ye ancient virgins lone,
From infancy to bag-and-muff so resolutely grown?

Each Sunday morning out you drove to Parson Arms's church,
As straight as if Time had not left you somehow in the lurch;
And so lived where your grandfather and father lived and died,
Until you sought them one by one — and last of all stayed pride.

You knew that with them you would lie in that old burial ground
Wherethrough the name of Huntington on vault and stone is found,
Where Norwichtown's first infant male, in sixteen-sixty born,
Grave Christopher, still rests beneath his cherub carved forlorn.

There sleep your warlike ancestors, their feet toward the east,

And thus shall face the Judgment Throne when
Gabriel's blast hath ceased.
The frost of years may heave the tomb whereto
you were consigned,
And school-boys peer atween the cracks, but you
— will never mind.

1894

CENTURIA

(TWELFTH NIGHT CHORUS, CENTURY ASSOCIATION)

THE burthen is all that there is of this song,
Centuria!
Let it sound through the halls where our memories throng—
Where thy dead and thy living commingled belong;
Centuria, Centuria, vivat Centuria!

Let it sound till the wise and the gentle and brave,
Centuria,
Come back from the vale where their soft grasses wave,
And list to our revel and join in the stave;
Centuria, Centuria, vivat Centuria!

For the pen, lute and gown, and the iris-hued sky,
Centuria,
Were theirs, and are ours while the nights still go by

With song, wit and wassail, and true hearts anigh.
Centuria, Centuria, vivat Centuria!

Then love as they loved when thine eldest was young,
Centuria!
O the comrades that gossipped and painted and sung,
O the smoke-cloud that lingers their places among!
Centuria, Centuria, vivat Centuria!

And sing as they 'll sing in thy fair years untold,
Centuria,
Strong hearts that shall follow, as tender and bold;
We may fade, we shall pass, but thou growest not old;
Centuria, Centuria, vivat Centuria!

1892

INSCRIPTIONS

I

THAT border land 'twixt Day and Night be mine,
And choice companions gathered there to dine,
With talk, song, mirth, soup, salad, bread and wine.

Twilight Club, 1883

II

AT set of sun one lone star rules the skies,
Night spreads a feast the day's long toil has won:
Eat, drink, — enough, no more, — and speak, ye wise,
Speak — but enough, no more, at set of sun!

Sunset Club, 1891

III

COMMEMORATIONS

THE DEATH OF BRYANT

How was it then with Nature when the soul
  Of her own poet heard a voice which came
From out the void, "Thou art no longer lent
To Earth!" when that incarnate spirit, blent
With the abiding force of waves that roll,
  Wind-cradled vapors, circling stars that flame,
        She did recall? How went
His antique shade, beaconed upon its way
Through the still aisles of night to universal day?

Her voice it was, her sovereign voice, which bade
  The Earth resolve his elemental mould;
And once more came her summons: "Long, too long,
Thou lingerest, and charmest with thy song!
Return! return!" Thus Nature spoke, and made
  Her sign; and forthwith on the minstrel old
        An arrow, bright and strong,

Fell from the bent bow of the answering Sun,
Who cried, "The song is closed, the invocation
done!"

But not as for those youths dead ere their prime,
New-entered on their music's high domain,
Then snatched away, did all things sorrow own:
No utterance now like that sad sweetest tone
When Bion died, and the Sicilian rhyme
Bewailed; no sobbing of the reeds that plain
Rehearsing some last moan
Of Lycidas; no strains which skyward swell
For Adonais still, and still for Asphodel!

The Muses wept not for him as for those
Of whom each vanished like a beauteous star
Quenched ere the shining midwatch of the night;
The greenwood Nymphs mourned not his lost de-
light;
Nor Echo, hidden in the tangled close,
Grieved that she could not mimic him afar.
He ceased not from our sight
Like him who, in the first glad flight of spring,
Fell as an eagle pierced with shafts from his own
wing.

This was not Thyrsis! no, the minstrel lone
And reverend, the woodland singer hoar,
Who was dear Nature's nursling, and the priest
Whom most she loved; nor had his office ceased
But for her mandate: "Seek again thine own;
The walks of men shall draw thy steps no more!"
Softly, as from a feast
The guest departs that hears a low recall,
He went, and left behind his harp and coronal.

"*Return!*" she cried, "unto thine own return!
Too long the pilgrimage; too long the dream
In which, lest thou shouldst be companionless,
Unto the oracles thou hadst access, —
The sacred groves that with my presence yearn."
The voice was heard by mountain, dell, and stream,
Meadow and wilderness —
All fair things vestured by the changing year,
Which now awoke in joy to welcome one most dear.

"*He comes!*" declared the unseen ones that haunt
The dark recesses, the infinitude

UofM

Of whispering old oaks and soughing pines.
"*He comes!*" the warders of the forest shrines
Sang joyously. "His spirit ministrant
  Henceforth with us shall walk the underwood,
      Till mortal ear divines
Its music added to our choral hymn,
Rising and falling far through archways deep and
      dim!"

The orchard fields, the hillside pastures green,
  Put gladness on; the rippling harvest-wave
Ran like a smile, as if a moment there
His shadow poised in the midsummer air
Above; the cataract took a pearly sheen
  Even as it leapt; the winding river gave
      A sound of welcome where
He came, and trembled, far as to the sea
It moves from rock-ribbed heights where its dark
      fountains be.

His presence brooded on the rolling plain,
  And on the lake there fell a sudden calm,—
His own tranquillity; the mountain bowed
Its head, and felt the coolness of a cloud,
And murmured, "*He is passing!*" and again

Through all its firs the wind swept like a psalm;
Its eagles, thunder-browed,
In that mist-moulded shape their kinsman knew,
And circled high, and in his mantle soared from view.

So drew he to the living veil, which hung
Of old above the deep's unimaged face,
And sought his own. Henceforward he is free
Of vassalage to that mortality
Which men have given a sepulchre among
The pathways of their kind, — a resting-place
Where, bending one great knee,
Knelt the proud mother of a mighty land
In tenderness, and came anon a plumèd band.

Came one by one the seasons meetly drest,
To sentinel the relics of their seer.
First Spring — upon whose head a wreath was set
Of wind-flowers and the yellow violet —
Advanced. Then Summer led his loveliest
Of months, one ever to the minstrel dear
(Her sweet eyes dewy wet),
June, and her sisters, whose brown hands entwine
The brier-rose and the bee-haunted columbine.

Next, Autumn, like a monarch sad of heart,
Came, tended by his melancholy days.
Purple he wore, and bore a golden rod,
His sceptre; and let fall upon the sod
A lone fringed-gentian ere he would depart.
Scarce had his train gone darkling down the ways
When Winter thither trod, —
Winter, with beard and raiment blown before,
That was so seeming like our poet old and hoar.

What forms are these amid the pageant fair,
Harping with hands that falter? What sad throng?
They wait in vain, a mournful brotherhood,
And listen where their laurelled elder stood
For some last music fallen through the air.
"What cold, thin atmosphere now hears thy song?"
They ask, and long have wooed
The woods and waves that knew him, but can learn
Naught save the hollow, haunting cry, "*Return! return!*"

1878

GIFFORD

I

THE CLOSED STUDIO

THIS was a magician's cell:
Beauty's self obeyed his spell!
When the air was gloom without,
Grace and Color played about
Yonder easel. Many a sprite,
Golden-winged with heaven's light,
Let the upper skies go drear,
Spreading his rare plumage here.

Skyward now, — alas the day! —
See the truant Ariels play!
Cloud and air with light they fill,
Wandering at idle will,
Nor (with half their tasks undone)
Stay to mourn the master gone.
Only in this hollow room,
Now, the stillness and the gloom.

II

OF WINTER NIGHTS

When the long nights return, and find us met
Where he was wont to meet us, and the flame
On the deep hearth-stone gladdens as of old,
And there is cheer, as ever in that place,
How shall our utmost nearing close the gap
Known, but till then scarce measured? Or what light
Of cheer for us, his gracious presence gone,
His speech delayed, till none shall fail to miss
That halting voice, yet sure, speaking, it seemed
The one apt word? For well the painter knew
Art's alchemy and law; her nobleness
Was in his soul, her wisdom in his speech,
And loyalty was housed in that true heart,
Gentle yet strong, and yielding not one whit
Of right or purpose. Now, not more afar
The light of last year's Yule fire than the smile
Of Gifford, nor more irreclaimable
Its vapor mingled with the wintry air.

1880

CORDA CONCORDIA

READ AT THE OPENING SESSION OF THE SUMMER SCHOOL OF PHILOSOPHY, CONCORD, JULY 11, 1881

No sandalled footsteps fall,
Tablet and coronal
From the Cephissian grove have vanished long,
Yet in the sacred dale
Still bides the nightingale
Easing his ancient heart-break still with song;
Or is there some dim audience
Viewless to all save his unclouded sense?

Revisit now those glades
The stately mantled shades
Whose lips so wear the inexorable spell?
Saying, with heads sunk low,
All that we sought, we know,—
We know, but not to mortal ears may tell:
No answer unto man's desire
Shall thus be made, to quench his eager fire.

Under these orchard trees
Still pure and fresh the breeze
As where the plane-tree whispered to the elm;[1]
The thrush and robin bring
A new-world offering
Of song, — nor are we banished from the realm
Of thought that as the wind is pure,
And converse deep, and memories that endure.

Some honey dropped as well,
Some dew of hydromel
From wilding meadow-bees, upon the lips
Of poet and sage who found,
Here on our own dear ground,
Light as of old; who let no dull eclipse
Obscure this modern sky, where first
Through perilous clouds the dawn of freedom burst.

Within this leafy haunt
Their service ministrant
Upheld the nobler freedom of the soul.
How was it hither came
The message and the flame
Anew? Make answer from thine aureole

[1] Aristophanes: Nubes, 995.

O mother Nature, thou who best
Man's heart in all thy ways interpretest!

High thoughts of thee brought near
Unto our minstrel-seer
The antique calm, the Asian wisdom old,
Till in his verse we heard
Of blossom, bee, and bird,
Of mountain crag and pine, the manifold
Rich song, — and on the world his eyes
Dwelt penetrant with vision sweet and wise.

Whence came the silver tongue
To one forever young
Who spoke until our hearts within us burned?
This reverend one, who took
No palimpsest or book,
But read his soul with glances inward turned,
While (her rapt forehead like the dawn)
The Sibyl listened, by that music drawn,

And from her fearless mouth,
Where never speech had drouth,
Gave voice to some old chant of womanhood, —
Her own imaginings,

Like swift, resplendent things,
Flashing from eyes that knew to beam or brood.
What sought these shining ones? What thought
From preacher-saint have poet and teacher caught?

In scorn of meaner use,
Anon, the young recluse
Builded his hut beside the woodland lake,
And set the world far off,
Though with no will to scoff,
Thus from the Earth's near breast fresh life to take.
Against her bosom, heart to heart,
All Nature's sweets he ravished for his Art.

The soul's fine instrument,
Of pains and raptures blent,
Replied to these clear voices, tone for tone,
Their cadence answering
With tuneful sounds that wing
The upper air a few perchance have known,
The stormless empyrean, where
In strength and joy a few move unaware.

Ah, even thus the thrill
Of life beyond life's ill

To feel betimes our envious selves are fain, —
Seeing that, as birds in night
Wind-driven against the light
Whose unseen armor mocks their stress and pain,
Most men fall baffled in the surge
That to their cry responds but with a dirge.

Where broods the Absolute,
Or shuns our long pursuit
By fiery utmost pathways out of ken?
Fleeter than sunbeams, lo,
Our passionate spirits go,
And traverse immemorial space, and then
Look off, and look in vain, to find
The master-clew to all they left behind.

White orbs like angels pass
Before the triple glass,
That men may scan the record of each flame, —
Of spectral line and line
The legendry divine, —
Finding their mould the same, and aye the same,
The atoms that we knew before
Of which ourselves are made, — dust, and no more.

So let our defter art
Probe the warm brain, and part
Each convolution of the trembling shell:
But whither now has fled
The sense to matter wed
That murmured here? All silence, such as fell
When to the shrine beyond the Ark
The soldiers reached, and found it void and dark.

Seek elsewhere, and in vain
The wings of morning chain;
Their speed transmute to fire, and bring the Light,
The co-eternal beam
Of the blind minstrel's dream;
But think not that bright heat to know aright,
Nor how the trodden seed takes root,
Waked by its glow, and climbs to flower and fruit.

Behind each captured law
Weird shadows give us awe;
Press with your swords, the phantoms still evade;
Through our alertest host
Wanders at ease some ghost,
Now here, now there, by no enchantment laid,
And works upon our souls its will,
Leading us on to subtler mazes still.

We think, we feel, we are;
And light, as of a star,
Gropes through the mist, — a little light is given;
And aye from life and death
We strive, with indrawn breath,
To somehow wrest the truth, and long have striven,
Nor pause, though book and star and clod
Reply, *Canst thou by searching find out God?*

As from the hollow deep
The soul's strong tide must keep
Its purpose still. We rest not, though we hear
No voice from heaven let fall,
No chant antiphonal
Sounding through sunlit clefts that open near;
We look not outward, but within,
And think not quite to end as we begin.

For now the questioning age
Cries to each hermitage,
Cease not to ask, — or bring again the time
When the young world's belief
Made light the mourner's grief
And strong the sage's word, the poet's rhyme, —
Ere Knowledge thrust a spear-head through
The temple's veil that priests so closely drew.

From what our fate inurns —
Save that which music yearns
To speak, in ecstasy none understand,
And (Oh, how like to it!)
The half-formed rays that flit,
Like memories vague, above the further land —
Cry, as the star-led Magi cried,
We seek, we seek, we will not be denied!

Let the blind throng await
A healer at the gate;
Our hearts press on to see what yonder lies,
Knowing that arch on arch
Shall loom across the march
And over portals gained new strongholds rise.
The search itself a glory brings,
Though foiled so oft, that seeks the soul of things.

Some brave discovery,
Howbeit in vain we try
To clutch the shape that lures us evermore,
It shall be ours to make, —
As, where the waters break
Upon the margin of a pathless shore,
They find, who sought for gold alone,
The sudden wonders of a clime unknown.

Such treasure by the way
Your errantry shall pay,
Nor shall it aught against your hope prevail
That not to waking eyes
The golden clouds arise
Wherewith our visions clothe the mystic Grail,
When, in blithe halts upon the road,
We sleep where pilgrims earlier gone abode.

After the twelvemonth set
When as of old they met,
(A twelvemonth and a day, and kept their tryst),
And knight to pilgrim told,
Things given them to behold
What country found, what gained of all they wist,
(While ministering hands assign
To each a share of healing food and wine,)

So come, — when long grass waves
Above the holiest graves
Of them whose ripe adventure chides our own, —
Come where the great elms lean
Their quivering leaves and green
To shade the moss-clung roofs now sacred grown,
And where the bronze and granite tell
How Liberty was hailed with Life's farewell.

Here let your Academe
Be no ignoble dream,
But, consecrate with life and death and song,
Through the land's spaces spread
The trust inherited,
The hope which from your hands shall take no wrong,
And build an altar that may last
Till heads now young be laurelled with the Past.

ON A GREAT MAN WHOSE MIND IS CLOUDING

That sovereign thought obscured? That vision clear
  Dimmed in the shadow of the sable wing,
  And fainter grown the fine interpreting
Which as an oracle was ours to hear!
Nay, but the Gods reclaim not from the seer
  Their gift, — although he ceases here to sing,
  And, like the antique sage, a covering
Draws round his head, knowing what change is near.

1882

ON THE DEATH OF AN INVINCIBLE SOLDIER

O what a sore campaign,
  Of which men long shall tell,
Ended when he was slain —
  When this our greatest fell!

For him no mould had cast
  A bullet surely sped;
No falchion, welded fast,
  His iron blood had shed.

Death on the hundredth field
  Had failed to bring him low;
He was not born to yield
  To might of mortal foe.

Even to himself unknown,
  He bore the fated sword,

Forged somewhere near His throne
  Of battles still the Lord.

That weapon when he drew,
  Back rolled the wrath of men,—
Their onset feebler grew,
  The Nation rose again.

The splendor and the fame—
  Whisper of these alone,
Nor say that round his name
  A moment's shade was thrown;

Count not each satellite
  'Twixt him and glory's sun,
The circling things of night;
  Number his battles won.

Where then to choose his grave?
  From mountain unto sea,
The Land he fought to save
  His sepulchre shall be.

Yet to its fruitful earth
His quickening ashes lend,
That chieftains may have birth,
And patriots without end.

His carven scroll shall read:
Here rests the valiant heart
Whose duty was his creed,—
Whose lot, the warrior's part.

Who, when the fight was done,
The grim last foe defied,
Naught knew save victory won,
Surrendered not — but died.

1885

MnU

LIBERTY ENLIGHTENING THE WORLD

WARDER at ocean's gate,
  Thy feet on sea and shore,
Like one the skies await
  When time shall be no more!
What splendors crown thy brow?
What bright dread angel Thou,
  Dazzling the waves before
    Thy station great?

"My name is Liberty!
  From out a mighty land
I face the ancient sea,
  I lift to God my hand;
By day in Heaven's light,
A pillar of fire by night,
  At ocean's gate I stand
    Nor bend the knee.

"The dark Earth lay in sleep,
  Her children crouched forlorn,
Ere on the western steep
  I sprang to height, reborn:
Then what a joyous shout
The quickened lands gave out,
  And all the choir of morn
    Sang anthems deep.

"Beneath yon firmament,
  The New World to the Old
My sword and summons sent,
  My azure flag unrolled:
The Old World's hands renew
Their strength; the form ye view
  Came from a living mould
    In glory blent.

"O ye, whose broken spars
  Tell of the storms ye met,
Enter! fear not the bars
  Across your pathway set;
Enter at Freedom's porch,
For you I lift my torch,
  For you my coronet
    Is rayed with stars.

"But ye that hither draw
To desecrate my fee,
Nor yet have held in awe
The justice that makes free,—
Avaunt, ye darkling brood!
By Right my house hath stood:
My name is Liberty,
My throne is Law."

O wonderful and bright,
Immortal Freedom, hail!
Front, in thy fiery might,
The midnight and the gale;
Undaunted on this base
Guard well thy dwelling-place:
Till the last sun grow pale
Let there be Light!

1888

AD VIGILEM

WHAT seest thou, where the peaks about thee stand,
  Far up the ridge that severs from our view
  That realm unvisited? What prospect new
Holds thy rapt eye? What glories of the land,
Which from yon loftier cliff thou now hast scanned,
  Upon thy visage set their lustrous hue?
  Speak, and interpret still, O Watchman true,
The signals answering thy lifted hand!

And bide thee yet! still linger, ere thy feet
  To sainted bards that beckon bear thee down —
Though lilies, asphodel and spikenard sweet
  Await thy tread to blossom; and the crown
Long since is woven of Heaven's palm-leaves, meet
  For him whom Earth can lend no more renown.

Whittier's Eightieth Birthday
December 17, 1887

"ERGO IRIS"

Weary at length of the ancestral gloom,
  The self-same drone, the patter of dull pens,
Nature sent Iris of the rosy plume,
  Bearing to Holmes her wonder-working lens;
Grateful, he gave his dearest child her name,
  Lit the shrewd East with laughter, love and
      tears, —
Bade halt the sun — and arching into fame
  His rainbowed fancy now the world enspheres.

On his Eightieth Birthday
August 29, 1889

W. W.

Good-bye, Walt!
Good-bye, from all you loved of earth —
Rock, tree, dumb creature, man and woman —
To you, their comrade human.
The last assault
Ends now; and now in some great world has birth
A minstrel, whose strong soul finds broader wings,
More brave imaginings.
Stars crown the hilltop where your dust shall lie,
Even as we say good-bye,
Good-bye, old Walt!

Lines sent to his funeral
with an ivy wreath,
March 30, 1892

BYRON

A HUNDRED years, 't is writ, — O presage vain! —
  Earth wills her offspring life, ere one complete
His term, and rest from travail, and be fain
  To lay him down in natural death and sweet.

What of her child whose swift divining soul
  With triple fervor burns the torch apace,
And in one radiant third compacts the whole
  Ethereal flame that lights him on his race?

Ay, what of him who to the winds upheld
  A star-like brand, with pride and joy and tears,
And lived in that fleet course from youth to eld,
  Count them who will, his century of years?

The Power that arches heaven's orbway round
  Gave to this planet's brood its soul of fire,

Its heart of passion, — and for life unbound
  By chain or creed the measureless desire;

Gave to one poet these, and manifold
  High thoughts, beyond our lesser mortal share, —
Gave dreams of beauty, yes, and with a mould
  The antique world had worshipped made him fair;

Then touched his lips with music, — lit his brow,
  Even as a fane upon a sunward hill,
For strength, gave scorn, the pride that would not bow,
  The glorious weapon of a dauntless will.

But that the surcharged spirit — a vapor pent
  In beetling crags — a torrent barriered long —
A wind 'gainst heaven's four winds imminent —
  Might memorably vent its noble song,

Each soaring gift was fretted with a band
  That deadlier clung which way he fain would press:

His were an adverse age, a sordid land,
  Gauging his heart by their own littleness;

Blind guides! the fiery spirit scorned their curb,
  And Byron's love and gladness, — such the wise
Of ministrants whom evil times perturb, —
  To wrath and melancholy changed their guise.

Yet this was he whose swift imaginings
  Engirt fair Liberty from clime to clime, —
From Alp to ocean with an eagle's wings
  Pursued her flight, in Harold's lofty rime.

Where the mind's freedom was not, could not be,
  That bigot soil he rendered to disdain,
And sought, like Omar in his revelry,
  At least the semblance of a joy to gain.

Laughter was at his beck, and wisdom's ruth
  Sore-learned from fierce experiences that test
Life's masquerade, the carnival of youth,
  The world of man. Then Folly lost her zest,

Yet left undimmed (her valediction sung
  With Juan's smiles and tears) his natal ray
Of genius inextinguishably young, —
  An Eôs through those mists proclaiming day.

How then, when to his ear came Hellas' cry,
  He shred the garlands of the wild night's feast,
And rose a chief, to lead — alas, to die
  And leave men mourning for that music ceased!

America! When nations for thy knell
  Listened, one prophet oracled thy part:
Now, in thy morn of strength, remember well
  The bard whose chant foretold thee as thou art.

Sky, mount, and forest, and high-sounding main,
  The storm-cloud's vortex, splendor of the day,
Gloom of the night, — with these abide his strain, —
  And these are thine, though he has passed away;

Their elemental force had roused to might
  Great Nature's child in this her realm supreme, —

From their commingling he had guessed aright
  The plenitude of all we know or dream.

Read thou aright his vision and his song,
  That this enfranchised spirit of the spheres
May know his name henceforth shall take no wrong,
  Outbroadening still yon ocean and these years!

1888

YALE ODE FOR COMMENCEMENT DAY

I

HARK! through the archways old
High voices manifold
Sing praise to our fair Mother, praise to Yale!
The Muses' rustling garments trail;
White arms, with myrtle and with laurel wound,
Bring crowns to her, the Crowned!
Youngest and blithest, and awaited long,
The heavenly maid, sweet Music's child divine,
With golden lyre and joy of choric song
Leads all the Sisters Nine.

II

In the gray of a people's morn,
In the faith of the years to be,
The sacred Mother was born
On the shore of the fruitful sea;

By the shore she grew, and the ancient winds of
the East
Made her brave and strong, and her beauteous youth
increased
Till the winds of the West, from a wondrous
land,
From the strand of the setting sun to the sea of
her sunrise strand,
From fanes which her own dear hand hath
planted in grove and mead and vale,
Breathe love from her countless sons of might to
the Mother — breathe praise to Yale.

III

Mother of Learning! thou whose torch
Starward uplifts, afar its light to bear, —
Thine own revere thee throned within thy porch,
Rayed with thy shining hair.
The youngest know thee still more young, —
The stateliest, statelier yet than prophet-bard hath
sung.
O mighty Mother, proudly set
Beside the far-inreaching sea,
None shall the trophied Past forget
Or doubt thy splendor yet to be!

1895

"UBI SUNT QUI ANTE NOS?"

READ AT THE SEMI-CENTENNIAL MEETING OF THE CENTURY ASSOCIATION, JANUARY 13, 1897

How now are the Others faring? Where sit
They all in state?
And is there a token that somewhere, beyond the
muffled gate,
The vanished and unreturning, whose names our
memories fill,
Are holding their upper conclave and are of the
Century still?

Is it all a fancy that somewhere, that somehow,
the mindful Dead,
From the first that made his exit to the latest kinsman
sped, —
Their vision ourselves unnoting, their shapes by
ourselves unseen, —
Have gathered like us, together this night in that
strange demesne?

That the astral world's telepathy along their aisles
of light
Has summoned our brave immortals, this selfsame
mortal night,
All in that rare existence where thoughts a sub-
stance are,
To their native planet's aura, from journeyings
near and far;

And that now with forms made over, and life as
jocund and young
As when they here kept wassail and joined in the
catches sung,
They have met in the ancient fashion, and now
in the old-time speech
Are chanting their Vivat Centuria just out of our
hearing's reach?

Yes, O yes, — as the pictured ghosts of Huns
war on in middle air
With a fiercer battle-hunger from the field up-
flinging there, —
And since the things we have chosen from all, as
most of worth
Forever here and hereafter, cease not with the end
of Earth;

Since joy and knowledge and beauty, and the love
of man to man
Passing the love of women, the links of our chain
began, —
Yea, even as these are ceaseless, so they who were
liegemen here
Hark back and are all Centurions this night of the
fiftieth year!

Yes, the draftsmen and craftsmen have fashioned
with a dream's compelling force
The Century's lordlier temple, have builded it
course on course,
And a luminiferous ether floods the great assembly-
hall
Where the scintillant "C. A." colophon burns
high in the sight of all.

The painters have hung from end to end cloud-
canvases ablaze
With that color-scheme from us hidden in the
ultra-violet rays,

With the new chiaroscuro of things that each way
 face,
And the in-and-out perspective of their four-dimen-
 sioned space.

O, to hear the famed Cantators upraise the mighty
 chant,
With their bass transposed to the rumbling depth
 below our octaves scant,
And a tenor of those Elysian notes "too fine for
 mortal ear,"
Yet tuned to the diapason of this dear old darkling
 sphere!

And O, to catch but a glimpse of the company
 thronged around—
The scholars that know it all at last, the poets
 finally crowned!
There the blithe divines, that fear no more the
 midnight chimes, sit each
With his halo tilted a trifle, and his harp at easy
 reach;

There all the jolly Centurions of high or low degree,
This night of nights, as in early time, foregather gloriously, —
Come back, mayhap, from Martian meads, from many an orb come back,
Full sure the cheer they cared for here this night shall have no lack;

For they know the jovial servitors have mingled a noble brew
Of the tipple men call nectarean, the pure celestial dew,
And are passing around ambrosial cakes, while the incense-clouds arise
Of something akin to those earthly fumes not even the Blest despise.

And yet — and yet — could we listen, we might o'erhear them say
They would barter a year of Aidenn to be here for a night and a day;
And if one of us yearns to follow the paths that thitherward wend —
Let him rest content, — let him have no fear, — he verily shall in the end.

Then not for the quick alone this hour unbar the
entrance gate,
But a health to the brethren gone before, however
they hold their state!
Nor think it all fancy that to our hearts there
comes an answering thrill
From the Dead that echo our Vivats and are of
the Century still.

IV

THE CARIB SEA

KENNST DU?

Do you know the blue of the Carib Sea
Far out where there 's nothing but sky to bound
The gaze to windward, the glance to lee, —
More deep than the bluest spaces be
Betwixt white clouds in heaven's round?
Have you seen the liquid lazuli spread
From edge to edge, so wondrous blue
That your footfall's trust it might almost woo,
Were it smooth and low for one to tread?
So clear and warm, so bright, so dark,
That he who looks on it can but mark
'T is a different tide from the far-away
Perpetual waters, old and gray,
And can but wonder if Mother Earth
Has given a younger ocean birth.

Do you know how surely the trade-wind blows
To west-sou'west, through the whole round year?
How, after the hurricane comes and goes,
For nine fair moons there is naught to fear?

How the brave wind carries the tide before
Its breath, and on to the southwest shore?
How the Caribbean billows roll,
One after the other, and climb forever, —
The yearning waves of a shoreless river
That never, never can reach its goal?
They follow, follow, now and for aye,
One after the other, brother and brother,
And their hollow crests half hide the play
Of light where the sun's red sword thrusts home;
But still in a tangled shining chain
They quiver and fall and rise again,
And far before them the wind-borne spray
Is shaken on from their froth and foam, —
And for leagues beyond, in gray and rose,
The sundown shimmering distance glows!
— So bright, so swift, so glad, the sea
That girts the isles of Caribbee.

Do you know the green of those island shores
By the morning sea-breeze fanned?
(The tide on the reefs that guard them roars —
Then slips by stealth to the sand.)
Have you found the inlet, cut between
Like a rift across the crescent moon,
And anchored off the dull lagoon
Close by forest fringes green, —

Cool and green, save for the lines
Of yellow cocoa-trunks that lean,
Each in its own wind-nurtured way,
And bend their fronds to the wanton vines
Beneath them all astray?

Here is no mangrove warp-and-woof
From which a vapor lifts aloof,
But on the beaches smooth and dry
Red-lipped conch-shells lie —
Even at the edge of that green wall
Where the shore-grape's tendriled runners spread
And purple trumpet-creepers fall,
And the frangipani's clusters shed
Their starry sweets withal.
The silly cactuses writhe around,
Yet cannot choose but in grace to mingle,
This side the twittering waters sound,
On the other opens a low green dingle,
And between your ship and the shore and sky
The frigate-birds like fates appear,
The flapping pelican feeds about,
The tufted cardinals sing and fly.
So fair the shore, one has no fear;
And the sailors, gathered forward, shout
With strange glad voices each to each, —
Though well the harbor's depth they know

And the craven shark that lurks below, —
"Ho! let us over, and strike out
Until we stand upon the beach,
Until that wonderland we reach!"
— So green, so fair, the island lies,
As if 't were adrift from Paradise.

SARGASSO WEED

Out from the seething Stream
  To the steadfast trade-wind's courses,
Over the bright vast swirl
  Of a tide from evil free, —
Where the ship has a level beam,
  And the storm has spent his forces,
And the sky is a hollow pearl
  Curved over a sapphire sea.

Here it floats as of old,
  Beaded with gold and amber,
Sea-frond buoyed with fruit,
  Sere as the yellow oak,
Long since carven and scrolled,
  Of some blue-ceiled Gothic chamber
Used to the viol and lute
  And the ancient belfry's stroke.

Eddying far and still
  In the drift that never ceases,

THE CARIB SEA

The dun Sargasso weed
  Slips from before our prow,
And its sight makes strong our will,
  As of old the Genoese's,
When he stood in his hour of need
  On the Santa Maria's bow.

Ay, and the winds at play
  Toy with these peopled islands,
Each of itself as well
  Naught but a brave New World,
Where the crab and sea-slug stay
  In the lochs of its tiny highlands,
And the nautilus moors his shell
  With his sail and streamers furled.

Each floats ever and on
  As the round green Earth is floating
Out through the sea of space
  Bearing our mortal kind,
Parasites soon to be gone,
  Whom others be sure are noting,
While to their astral race
  We in our turn are blind.

CASTLE ISLAND LIGHT

I

BETWEEN the outer Keys,
  Where the drear Bahamas be,
Through a crooked pass the vessels sail
  To reach the Carib Sea.

'T is the Windward Passage, long and dread,
  From bleak San Salvador;
(Three thousand miles the wave must roll
  Ere it wash the Afric shore).

Here are the coral reefs
  That hold their booty fast;
The sea-fan blooms in groves beneath,
  And sharks go lolling past.

Hither and yon the sand-bars lie
  Where the prickly bush has grown,

And where the rude sponge-fisher dwells
   In his wattled hut, alone.

Southward, amid the strait,
   Is the Castle Island Light;
Of all that bound the ocean round
   It has the loneliest site.

II

'Twixt earth and heaven the waves are driven
   Sorely upon its flank;
The light streams out for sea-leagues seven
   To the Great Bahama Bank.

A girded tower, a furlong scant
   Of whitened sand and rock,
And one sole being the waters seeing,
   Where the gull and gannet flock.

He is the warder of the pass
   That mariners must find;
His beard drifts down like the ashen moss
   Which hangs in the southern wind.

The old man hoar stands on the shore
   And bodes the withering gale,
Or wonders whence from the distant world
   Will come the next dim sail.

From the Northern Main, from England,
   From France, the craft go by;
Yet sometimes one will stay her course
   That must his wants supply.

III

In a Christmas storm the "Claribel" struck
   At night, on the Pelican Shoal,
But the keeper's wife heard not the guns
   And the bell's imploring toll.

She died ere the gale went down,
   Wept by her daughters three—
Sun-flecked, yet fair, with their English hair,
   Nymphs of the wind and sea.

With sail and oar some island shore
   At will their skiffs might gain,

But they never had known the kiss of man,
  Nor had looked on the peopled main,

Nor heard of the old man Atlas,
  Who holds the unknown seas,
And the golden fruit that is guarded well
  By the young Hesperides.

IV

Who steers by Castle Island Light
  May hear the seamen tell
How one, the mate, alone was saved
  From the wreck of the "Claribel;"

And how for months he tarried
  With the keeper on the isle,
And for each of the blue-eyed daughters
  Had ever a word or a smile.

Between the two that loved him
  He lightly made his choice,

And betimes a chance ship took them off
   From the father's sight and voice.

The second her trouble could not bear,—
   So wild her thoughts had grown
That she fled with a lurking smuggler's crew,
   But whither was never known.

Then the keeper aged like Lear,
   Left with one faithful child;
But 't was ill to see a maid so young
   Who never sang or smiled.

'T is sad to bide with an old, old man,
   And between the wave and sky
To watch all day the sea-fowl play,
   While lone ships hasten by.

V

There came, anon, the white full moon
   That rules the middle year,

Before whose sheen the lesser stars
   Grow pale and disappear.

It glistened down on a lighthouse tower,
   A beach on either hand,
And the features wan of a gray old man
   Digging a grave in the sand.

CHRISTOPHE

(CAPE HAYTIEN)

"King Henri is King Stephen's peer,
His breeches cost him but a crown!"
So from the old world came the jeer
Of them who hunted Toussaint down:
But what was this grim slave that swept
The shambles, then to greatness leapt?
Their counterfeit in bronze, a thing
To mock, — or every inch a king?

On San-Souci's defiant wall
His people saw, against the sky,
Christophe, — a shape the height of Saul, —
A chief who brooked no rivals nigh.
Right well he aped the antique state;
His birth was mean, his heart was great;
No azure filled his veins, — instead,
The Afric torrent, hot and red.

He built far up the mountain-side
  A royal keep, and walled it round
With towers the palm-tops could not hide;
  The ramparts toward ocean frowned;
Beneath, within the rock-hewn hold,
He heaped a monarch's store of gold;
He made his nobles in a breath;
He held the power of life and death;

And here through torrid years he ruled
  The Haitian horde, a despot king,—
Mocked Europe's pomp,—her minions schooled
  In trade and war and parleying,—
Yet reared his dusky heirs in vain:
To end the drama, Fate grew fain,
Uprose a rebel tide, and flowed
Close to the threshold where he strode.

"And now the Black must exit make,
  A craven at the last," they say:
Not so,—Christophe his leave will take
  The long unwonted Roman way.
"Ho! Ho!" cried he, "the day is done,
And I go down with the setting sun!"
A pistol-shot,—no sign of fear,—
So died Christophe without a peer.

LA SOURCE

(PORT-AU-PRINCE)

A HAUNT the mountain roadside near,
Wherefrom the cliff that rose behind
Kept back, through all the tropic year,
The sundrouth and the whirling wind:
These here could never entrance find;
Perpetual summer balm it knew;
And skyward, thick-set boughs entwined
Their coil, where birds made sweet ado,
And heaven through glossy leaves was deepest
blue.

Twin relics of some forest grim,
The last of their primeval race
Left scatheless, knit them limb with limb
Above the reaches of that place;
Time's hand against their high embrace
For seeming centuries had striven,
But yet they grappled face to face,

Still from their olden guard undriven
Though at their feet the cliff itself was riven.

And from the rift a stream outflowed,
The fountain of that cloven grot, —
La Source ! Along the downward road
It speeded, pitying the lot
Of dwellers in each hot-roofed spot
Which fiery noonday held in rule, —
Yet at the start neglected not
To broaden into one deep pool
Beneath those trees its staunchless waters cool.

Near the green edge of this recess
We made our halt, and marvelled, more
Than at its sudden loveliness,
To find reborn that life of yore
When ocean to Nausicaa bore
The wanderer from Calypso strayed, —
For here swart dames, and beldames hoar,
With many a round-limbed supple maid,
Plashed in the pool and eyed us unafraid.

The simple, shameless washers there,
Dusk children of the Haitian sun,

Bent to the work their bodies, bare
And brown, nor thought our gaze to shun,—
Save that an elfish withered one,
Scolding the white-toothed girls, set free
Her tongue, and bade them now have done
With saucy pranks, nor wanton be
Before us stranger folk from over sea.

But on the sward one rose full length
From her sole covering, and stood
Defiant in the beauteous strength
Of nature unabashed: a nude
And wilding slip of womanhood.
Now for the master-hand, that shaped
The Indian Hunter in his wood,
To mould that lissome form undraped
Ere from its grace the sure young lines escaped!

Straight as the aloe's crested shoot
That blooms a golden month and dies,
She stayed an instant, with one foot
On tiptoe, poising statue-wise,
And stared, and mocked us with her eyes,—
While rippling to her hip's firm swell
The mestee hair, that so outvies

Europe's soft mesh, and holds right well
The Afric sheen, in one dark torrent fell.

Fi, Angélique! we heard them scream,—
What, could that child, in twice her years,
Change to their like from this fair dream!
Fi donc! — But she, as one who hears
And cares not, at her leisure nears
The pool, and toward her mates at play
Plunges, — and laughter filled our ears
As from La Source we turned away
And rode again into the glare of day.

TO L. H. S.

Love, these vagrant songs may woo you
      Once again from winter's ruth, —
Once more quicken memories failing
Of those days when we went sailing,
Eager as when first I knew you,
      Sailing after my lost youth.

My lost youth, for in my sight you
      Had yourself forborne to change
Since that age when we, together,
Made such mock of wind and weather,
Sought alone what might delight you, —
      Ah, how sweet, how far, how strange!

Yet, though scarcely else anear you
      Than Tithonus to Aurore,
I am still by Time requited,
Still can vaunt, as when we plighted,

Sight to see you, ear to hear you,
      Voice to sing you, if no more.

And in thought I yet behold you
      Nearing the enchanted zone, —
(With delight of life the stronger
As we sailed, each blue league longer,
Toward the shore of which I told you,
      And the stars myself had known), —

Wondering at the hue beneath you
      Of the restless shining waves,
Asking of the palm and coral, —
Of the white cascades — the floral
Ridges waiting long to wreathe you
      With the blooms our Norseland craves.

Winds enow since then have kissed you,
      On their way to bless or blight;
Little may these songs recover
Of that dream-life swiftly over, —
Nay, but Love, a moment list you,
      Since none else can set them right.

TO L. H. S.

More and ever more, the while you
    Sailed where every distance gleams,
Passed all sorrow, died all anger,
In the clime of love and languor,
Till we reached the mist-hung isle you
    Called the haunted Isle of Dreams.

JAMAICA

I KNOW an island which the sun
Stays in his course to shine upon,
As if it were for this green isle
Alone he kept his fondest smile.
Long his rays delaying flood
Its remotest solitude,
Mountain, dell, and palmy wood,
And the coral sands around
That hear the blue sea's chiming sound.

It is a watered island, one
The upland rains pour down upon.
Oft the westward-floating cloud
To some purple crest is bowed,
While the tangled vapors seek
To escape from peak and peak,
Yield themselves, and break, or glide
Through deep forests undescried,
Mourning their lost pathway wide.

JAMAICA

In this land of woods and streams
Ceaseless Summer paints her dreams:
White, bewildered torrents fall,
Dazzled by her morning beams,
With an outcry musical
From the ridges, plainward all;
Mists of pearl, arising there,
Mark their courses in the air,
Sunlit, magically fair.

Here the pilgrim may behold
How the bended cocoa waves
When at eve and morn a breeze
Blows to and from the Carib seas,
How the lush banana leaves
From their braided trunk unfold;
How the mango wears its gold,
And the sceptred aloe's bloom
Glorifies it for the tomb.

When the day has ended quite,
Splendor fills the drooping skies;
All is beauty, naught is night.
Then the Crosses twain arise,
Southward far, above the deep,

And the moon their light outvies.
Hark! the wakened lute and song
That to this fond clime belong, —
All is music, naught is sleep.

Isle of plenty, isle of love!
In the low, encircling plain
Laboring Afric, loaded wain,
Bearing sweets and spices, move;
On the happy heights above
Love his seat has chosen well,
Dreamful ease and silence dwell,
Life is all entranced, and time
Passes like a tinkling rhyme.

Ah, on those cool heights to dwell
Yielded to the island's spell!
There from some low-whispering mouth
To learn the secret of the South,
Or to watch dark eyes that close
When their sleep the noondays bring,
(List, the palm leaves murmuring!)
And the wind that comes and goes
Smells of every flower that blows.

Or from ocean to descry
Green plantations sloping nigh,
Starry peaks, of beryl hewn,
Whose strong footholds hidden lie
Furlong deep beneath the sea!
Long the mariners wistfully
Landward gaze, and say aright,
"Under sun or under moon
Earth has no more beauteous sight!"

CREOLE LOVER'S SONG

NIGHT wind, whispering wind,
    Wind of the Carib sea!
The palms and the still lagoon
Long for thy coming soon;
But first my lady find:
Hasten, nor look behind!
    To-night Love's herald be.

The feathery bamboo moves,
    The dewy plantains weep;
From the jasmine thickets bear
The scents that are swooning there,
And steal from the orange groves
The breath of a thousand loves
    To waft her ere she sleep.

And the lone bird's tender song
    That rings from the ceiba tree,
The firefly's light, and the glow

Of the moonlit waters low,—
All things that to night belong
And can do my love no wrong
    Bear her this hour for me.

Speed thee, wind of the deep,
    For the cyclone comes in wrath!
The distant forests moan;
Thou hast but an hour thine own,—
An hour thy tryst to keep,
Ere the hounds of tempest leap
    And follow upon thy path.

Whisperer, tarry a space!
    She waits for thee in the night;
She leans from the casement there
With the star-blooms in her hair,
And a shadow falls like lace
From the fern-tree over her face,
    And over her mantle white.

Spirit of air and fire,
    To-night my herald be!
Tell her I love her well,

And all that I bid thee, tell,
And fold her ever the nigher
With the strength of my soul's desire,
Wind of the Carib sea!

THE ROSE AND THE JASMINE

Now dies the rippling murmur of the strings
That followed long, half-striving to retake,
The burden of the lover's ended song.
Silence! but we who listened linger yet,
Two of the soul's near portals still unclosed —
Sight and the sense of odor. At our feet,
Beneath the open jalousies, is spread
A copse of leaf and bloom, a knotted wild
Of foliage and purple flowering vines,
With here a dagger-plant to pierce them through,
And there a lone papaya lifting high
Its golden-gourded cresset. Night's high noon
Is luminous; that swooning silvery hour
When the concentrate spirit of the South
Grows visible — so rare, and yet so filled
With tremulous pulsation that it seems
All light and fragrance and ethereal dew.

Two vases — carved from some dark, precious
wood,
The red-grained heart of olden trees that cling

To yonder mountain — in the moonlight cast
Their scrolls' deep shadows on the glassy floor.
A proud exotic Rose, brought from the North,
Is set within the one; the other bears
A double Jasmine for its counter-charm.
Here on their thrones, in equal high estate,
The rivals bloom; and both have drunk the dew,
Tending their beauty in the midnight air,
Until their sovereign odors meet and blend,
As voices blend that whisper melody,
Now each distinct, now mingled both in one:

JASMINE

I, like a star, against the woven gloom
  Of tresses on Dolores' brow shall rest.

ROSE

And I one happy, happy night shall bloom
  Twined in the border of her silken vest.

JASMINE

Throughout our isle the guardian winds deprive
  Of all their sweets a hundred common flowers,

To feed my heart with fragrance! Lone they
    live,
  And drop their petals far from trellised bowers.

ROSE

Within the garden-plot whence I was borne
  No rifled sisterhood became less fine;
My wealth made not the violet forlorn,
  And near me climbed the fearless eglantine.

JASMINE

Who feels my breath recalls the orange court,
  The terraced walks that jut upon the sea,
The water in the moonlit bay amort,
  The midnight given to longing and to me.

ROSE

Who scents my blossoms dreams of bordered
    meads
  Deep down the hollow of some vale far north,
Where Cuthbert with the fair-haired Hilda pleads,
  And overhead the stars of June come forth.

JASMINE

Me with full hands enamored Manuel
  Gathers for dark-browed Inez at his side,
And both to love are quickened by my spell,
  And chide the day that doth their joys divide.

ROSE

Nay, but all climes, all tender sunlit lands
  From whose high places spring the palm or pine,
Desire my gifts to grace the wedded bands,
  And every home for me has placed a shrine.

JASMINE

Fold up thy heart, proud virgin, ay, and blush
  With all the crimson tremors thou canst vaunt!
My yearning waves of passion onward rush,
  And long the lover's wistful memory haunt.

ROSE

Pale temptress, the night's revel be thine own,
  Till love shall pall and rapture have its fill!

THE ROSE AND THE JASMINE

The morn's fresh light still finds me on a throne
Where care is not, nor blissful pains that kill.

JASMINE

Sweet, sweet my breath, oh, sweet beyond compare!

ROSE

Rare, rare the splendors of my regal crown!

BOTH

Choose which thou wilt, bold lover, yet beware
Lest to a luckless choice thou bendest down!

FERN-LAND

I

HITHER, where a woven roof
Keeps the prying sun aloof
        From wonderland,
From the fairies underland,—
Hither, where strange grasses grow
With their curling rootlets set
'Twixt the black roots serpentine,
Laurel roots that twist and twine
Toward the cloven path below
Of some cloud-born rivulet,—
    This way enter
Fern-Land, and from rim to centre
All its secrets shall be thine.

II

Here within the covert see
Fern-Land's mimic forestry;
        Royal tree-ferns

Canopy the nestling wee ferns
That with every pointed frond
Lend their lords a duteous ear;
Golden ferns a sunshine make —
Fleck their beauty on the brake;
In their moonlight close beyond
Silver ferns like sprites appear.
        Here beholden,
Purple, silver, green and golden,
Mingle for their own sweet sake.

III

Day's sure horologe of flowers
Marks in turn the honeyed hours;
        Blossoms dangle,
Lithe lianas twist and tangle;
Here on the lagetta tree
Laboring elves at starlight weave
Filmy bride-veils of its spray,
Shot with the cocuya's ray, —
For in fairy-land we be!
Look, and you shall well believe
        Oberon reigneth,
And Titania disdaineth,
Still, to yield her lord his way.

IV

Here, unseen by grosser light,
Fairy-land, at noon of night
        Holidaying,
Sallies forth in fine arraying;
Elfin, sylphide, fay and gnome
On the dew-tipped ferns disport,
In the festooned creepers swing,
Their light plumage fluttering.
Fern-Land is their ancient home,
Here the monarch holds his court,
        Puck abideth;
Here the Queen her changeling hideth,
Ariel doth merrily sing.

V

Here, when Dian shuns the sky,
Swift the winged watchmen fly, —
        Flash their torches
In and out mimosa porches
Till the first pale glint of morn:
Then the little people change
Casque and doublet, robe and sash,
In the twinkling of a lash,

For the magic mantles worn
Warily where mortals range,
        And beside us
Now unseen, with glee deride us,
Laugh to scorn our trespass rash.

VI

Then the gnomes, that change to newts,
Lurk about the tree-fern's roots;
        Their commander
Is the frog-mouthed salamander
Who will marshal in the sun
Red-backed lizards from the vines,
Eft and newt from bog and spring,—
Many a crested, horny thing
Sharp-eyed, fearsome,—and that one
With the loathly spotted lines!
        Mortal heedeth
Him, whose breath of poison speedeth
Them that chafe the elfin king.

VII

Moths above, that feed on dew,
Flit their wings of gold and blue,—

Fancy guesses
These must be the court-princesses:
Others are in durance pent,
Changed to orchids for their tricks,—
Wantons they, who must remain
All day long in beauteous pain
Till stern Oberon relent,
Pardon grant, and seal affix.
Each repineth
Thus until the monarch dineth
And, content, doth loose her chain.

VIII

Would you had the fine, fine ear
The dragonfly's recall to hear,—
Tiny words
Of the vibrant humming-birds
That, where bloom convolvuli,
Round the dew-cups whir and hover,
Thrusting each, hour after hour,
His keen bill to heart o' the flower,
As some mounted knight may ply
His long lance, an eager lover,
Through deep sedges,
And athrough the coppice edges,
Fain to reach his lady's bower.

IX

Whilst the emerald lancers poise
In the soft air without noise,
        Brake and mould
Hoard their marvels manifold.
There the armored beetles creep,
Shrouding in unseemly fear
Each his shield of chrysoprase
Lest its gleam himself betrays
For our kind to seize and keep
Prisoned in a damsel's ear.
        Each one stealeth
Dumbly, and his dull way feeleth
Until starlight shall appear.

X

Step you soft, be mute and wary
Lest you wake the lords of Faery!
        Motion rude
Fits not with their solitude:
Else the spider will resent
And the beetle nip you well,
Bête-rouge in your neck will furrow,
Garapata dig his burrow: —

Dread the wasp's swift punishment
And the chegoe's vengeance fell:
    Well-defended,
Fairies sleep till day hath ended,—
Leave we Fern-Land and its spell.

MORGAN

Oh, what a set of Vagabundos,
  Sons of Neptune, sons of Mars,
Raked from todos otros mundos,
  Lascars, Gascons, Portsmouth tars,
Prison mate and dock-yard fellow,
  Blades to Meg and Molly dear,
Off to capture Porto Bello
  Sailed with Morgan the Buccaneer!

Out they voyaged from Port Royal
  (Fathoms deep its ruins be,
Pier and convent, fortress loyal,
  Sunk beneath the gaping sea);
On the Spaniard's beach they landed,
  Dead to pity, void of fear, —
Round their blood-red flag embanded,
  Led by Morgan the Buccaneer.

Dawn till dusk they stormed the castle,
  Beat the gates and gratings down;

Then, with ruthless rout and wassail,
  Night and day they sacked the town,
Staved the bins its cellars boasted,
  Port and Lisbon, tier on tier,
Quaffed to heart's content, and toasted
  Harry Morgan the Buccaneer:

Stripped the church and monastery,
  Racked the prior for his gold,
With the traders' wives made merry,
  Lipped the young and mocked the old,
Diced for hapless señoritas
  (Sire and brother bound anear), —
Juanas, Lolas, Manuelitas,
  Cursing Morgan the Buccaneer.

Lust and rapine, flame and slaughter,
  Forayed with the Welshman grim:
"Take my pesos, spare my daughter!"
  "Ha! ha!" roared that devil's limb,
"These shall jingle in our pouches,
  She with us shall find good cheer."
"Lash the graybeard till he crouches!"
  Shouted Morgan the Buccaneer.

Out again through reef and breaker,
While the Spaniard moaned his fate,
Back they voyaged to Jamaica,
Flush with doubloons, coins of eight,
Crosses wrung from Popish varlets,
Jewels torn from arm and ear, —
Jesu! how the Jews and harlots
Welcomed Morgan the Buccaneer!

CAPTAIN FRANCISCA

Off Maracaibo's wall
The squadron lay:
The dykes are carried all
With storm and shout!
Le Basque and Lolonnois
On land their crews deploy,
Through all that ruthless day
The Spaniards rout.

They sack the captured town
Ere set of sun;
Their blood-red pennons crown
The convent tower:
Then Du Plessis, the bold,
Cries: "Take my share of gold!
For me this pretty one,
This cloister flower!"

Dice, drink, and song, the while
They seek anew

The filibusters' isle,
    Tortuga's port.
Swift was the craft that bore
Francisca from her shore;
  Red-handed were its crew
    And grim their sport.

Unbraided fell her hair,
  A tropic cloud;
Seven days, with sob and prayer,
    She mourned the dead;
Like rain her tears fell;
But Du Plessis right well
  By saint and relic vowed
    As on they sped.

Ere past the Mer du Nord
  She smiled apace;
Her dark eyes evermore
    Sought his alone.
Hot wooed the Chevalier;
His outlaw-priest was near:
  Forsworn were home and race,
    She was his own.

Now cruel Lolonnois
  And fierce Le Basque
Unlade with wolfish joy
    The cargazon;
Land all their ribald braves,
Captives and naked slaves,
  With many a bale and cask,
    By rapine won;

Armor and altar-plate
  Brought over sea:
Pesos, a countless weight,
    The horde divide—
To each an equal share,
Else blades are in the air!
  Cries Du Plessis: "For me,
    My ship, and bride!"

They sailed the Mer du Nord,
  The Carib Sea,
Whose galleons fled before
    The Frenchman's crew;
But, in one deadly fight,
A swivel aimed aright
  Brought down young Du Plessis,
    Shot through and through.

Wild heart of France, in pride
  And ruin bred!
Against a heart he died,
    As brave, as free.
Sternly she bade his men
First sink the prize, and then
  Name one that in his stead
    Their chief should be.

Each red-shirt laid his hand
  Upon the Cross,
Swearing, at her command,
    Vengeance to wreak;
To scour the blue sea there
And seek the Spaniards' lair,
  From Gracias à Dios
    To Porto Rique.

His corse the deep she gave,
  Her life to hate;
Upon the land and wave
    Brought sudden fear:
No bearded Capitan,
Since first their woes began
  (The orphaned niñas prate),
    Cost them so dear!

From Maracaibo's Bay
  Anon put out
A frigate to waylay
    This ranger dark.
It crossed the Mer du Nord,
And, off San Salvador,
  Stayed, with defiance stout,
    Francisca's barque.

They grappled stern and prow
  Till the guns kissed!
Girt like her rovers, now
    She bids them board:
The first her blade had shorn
Was her own brother born.
  Blindly she smote, nor wist
    Whose life-stream poured.

Yet, as he fell, one ball
  His sure aim sped.
Her lips the battle-call
    Essay in vain.
Then deathful stroke on stroke,
Curses and powder-smoke,
  And blood like water shed
    Above the twain!

No quarter give or take!
The decks are gore;
Fresh gaps the Spaniards make,
Charging anew:
"Death to the buccaneer!
No more our fleet shall fear,
That sails the Mer du Nord,
This corsair crew!"

— On thy lone strand was made,
San Salvador,
One grave where two were laid
For bane or boon!
The last of all their race,
To each an equal place.
Guards well that sombre shore
The still lagoon.

PANAMA

Two towers the old Cathedral lifts
 Above the sea-walled town, —
The wild pine bristles from their rifts,
 The runners dangle down;
In either turret, staves in hand,
All day the mongrel ringers stand
And sound, far over bay and land,
 The Bells of Panama.

Loudly the cracked bells, overhead,
 Of San Francisco ding,
With Santa Ana, La Merced,
 Felípe, answering;
Banged all at once, and four times four,
Morn, noon, and night, the more and more
Clatter and clang with huge uproar
 The Bells of Panama.

From out their roosts the bellmen see
 The red-tiled roofs below, —

The Plaza folk that lazily
  To mass and cockpit go, —
Then pound afresh, with clamor fell,
Each ancient, broken, thrice-blest bell,
Till thrice our mouths have cursed as well
  The Bells of Panama.

The Cordillera guards the main
  As when Pedrarias bore
The cross, the castled flag of Spain,
  To the Pacific shore;
The tide still ebbs a league from quay,
The buzzards scour the emptied Bay:
"There 's a heretic to singe to-day, —
Come out! Come out!" — still strive to say
  The Bells of Panama.

MARTINIQUE IDYL

Love, the winds long to lure you to their home,
  To tempt you on beneath the northern arch!
There, in the swift, bright summer, you and I
May loiter where the elms' deep shadows lie;
There, by our household fire, bid Yule-tide come,
  And winter's cold, and every gust of March.

Stay, O stay with me here, and chasten
  Your heart still longing to wander more!
Ever the restless winds are winging,
But the white-plumed egrets, skyward-springing,
Over our blue sea hover, and hasten
  To light anew on their own dear shore.

The lips grow tired of honey, the cloyed ear
  Of music, and of light the eyelids tire.
I weary of the sky's eternal balm,
The ceaseless droop and rustle of the palm;
Only your whisper, love, constrains me here
  From that brave clime I would you might desire.

Cold, ah, cold is the sky, and leaden,
There where earth rounds off to the pole!
Still by kisses the moments number, —
Here are sweetness, and rest, and slumber,
All to lighten and naught to deaden
The heart's low murmur, the captured soul.

Dear, I would have you yearn, amid these sweets,
For the clear breeze that blows from waters gray, —
For some fresh, northern hill-top, overgrown
With bush and bloom and brake to you unknown;
There, while the hidden thrush his song repeats,
The rose shall tinge your cheek the livelong day.

Stay in the clime where living is loving
And the lips make music unaware;
Where copses thrill with the wood-doves' cooing,
And astral moths on the flight are wooing;
While the light colibris poise unmoving, —
Winged Loves that mate in the trembling air.

Nay, love itself will languish in the days
When Summer never doffs his burning helm.

No lasting links to bind the soul are wrought
Where passion takes no deeper cast from thought;
Ah! lend your ear a moment to the lays
   Our poets sing you of a trustier realm!

Under the cocoa-fronds that flutter,
   Here, where the lush white trumpet-flower
And the curled lianas roof us over,
So that no evil thing discover
The sighs we mingle, the words we utter,—
   Here, oh here, let us make our bower!

Love is not perfect, sweet, that like a dream
   Flows on without a forecast or a pain;
Some burden must betide to make it strong,
Some toil, to make its briefest bliss seem long,—
Ay, longer than the crossing of a stream
   Mist-haunted, lit by moons that surely wane.

Here, for a round of moons unbroken,
   A spell that holds shall your loss requite;
The fleet, sweet moments shall pass unreckoned
And all to our constant love be second,
And the fragrant lily shall be our token,
   That folds itself on the waves at night.

MARTINIQUE IDYL

Yonder, or here, and whether summer's star
  Burn overhead, or rains of autumn fall!

Or snows of winter in the frozen North?

Love, never doubt it!

Take me with you forth!
And oh, forget not in that land afar,
  I am your summer, — you, my life, my all!

ASTRA CAELI

Over the Carib Sea to-night
The stars hang low and near
From the inexplicable dome, —
Nearer, more close to sight,
Than from the skies which bound the stern gray sea
That girts our northern home.

Aftward the sister Crosses be,
And yonder to the lee
One burning cresset glows — a sphere
With light beyond a new moon's rays,
As if some world of vanished souls shone clear
And straight before our gaze.

Were now his spirit bright, —
Not veiled, nor dumb, —
My brother's, with the smile of years ago,

Hither to glide far down that path of light,
And lift a hand, and say aright, —
“Thou too shalt know
The orb from which I come!”

— Were thus ’twixt star and wave
His voice to reach me on the night-wind’s breath,
I would not lightly leave thee, Dear,
Nor them who with thee here
Make of Life’s best for me the choice and sum, —
But yet might not bemoan me, as the slave
Condemned, who hears the call to death;
For that strange heralding
Even of itself would answer all, — would prove
Life but a voyage such as this, and bring
To our adventuring
Its gage of the immortal boon,
Promise of after joy and toil and love;
And I would yield me, as the bird takes wing
Knowing its mate must follow sure and soon.

Ay, — but the trackless spirit
Comes not, nor is there utterance or sign
Of all we would divine
Vouchsafed from the unanswering dome:

No presence east or west, —
Only the stars — the restless wondering sea
Bearing us back, from foam-tipped crest to crest,
Toward the one small part ourselves inherit
Of this lone darkling world — and call our home.

V

ARIEL

IN MEMORY OF PERCY BYSSHE SHELLEY: BORN ON THE FOURTH OF AUGUST, A. D., 1792

ARIEL

WERT thou on earth to-day, immortal one,
How wouldst thou, in the starlight of thine eld,
The likeness of that morntide look upon
Which men beheld?
How might it move thee, imaged in time's glass,
As when the tomb has kept
Unchanged the face of one who slept
Too soon, yet moulders not, though seasons come and pass?

Has Death a wont to stay the soul no less?
And art thou still what SHELLEY was erewhile, —
A feeling born of music's restlessness —
A child's swift smile
Between its sobs — a wandering mist that rose
At dawn — a cloud that hung
The Euganéan hills among;
Thy voice, a wind-harp's strain in some enchanted close?

Thyself the wild west wind, O boy divine,
Thou fain wouldst be, — the spirit which in its breath
Wooes yet the seaward ilex and the pine
That wept thy death?
Or art thou still the incarnate child of song
Who gazed, as if astray
From some uncharted stellar way,
With eyes of wonder at our world of grief and wrong?

Yet thou wast Nature's prodigal; the last
Unto whose lips her beauteous mouth she bent
An instant, ere thy kinsmen, fading fast,
Their lorn way went.
What though the faun and oread had fled?
A tenantry thine own,
Peopling their leafy coverts lone,
With thee still dwelt as when sweet Fancy was not dead;

Not dead as now, when we the visionless,
In nature's alchemy more woeful wise,
Say that no thought of us her depths possess, —
No love, her skies.

ARIEL

Not ours to parley with the whispering June,
The genii of the wood,
The shapes that lurk in solitude,
The cloud, the mounting lark, the wan and waning moon.

For thee the last time Hellas tipped her hills
With beauty; India breathed her midnight moan,
Her sigh, her ecstasy of passion's thrills,
To thee alone.
Such rapture thine, and the supremer gift
Which can the minstrel raise,
Above the myrtle and the bays,
To watch the sea of pain whereon our galleys drift.

Therefrom arose with thee that lyric cry,
Sad cadence of the disillusioned soul
That asks of heaven and earth its destiny, —
Or joy or dole.
Wild requiem of the heart whose vibratings,
With laughter fraught, and tears,
Beat through the century's dying years
While for one more dark round the old Earth plumes her wings.

No answer came to thee; from ether fell
No voice, no radiant beam; and in thy youth
How were it else, when still the oracle
Withholds its truth?
We sit in judgment, — we, above thy page
Judge thee and such as thee,
Pale heralds, sped too soon to see
The marvels of our late yet unanointed age!

The slaves of air and light obeyed afar
Thy summons, Ariel; their elf-horns wound
Strange notes which all uncapturable are
Of broken sound.
That music thou alone couldst rightly hear
(O rare impressionist!)
And mimic. Therefore still we list
To its ethereal fall in this thy cyclic year.

Be then the poet's poet still! for none
Of them whose minstrelsy the stars have blessed
Has from expression's wonderland so won
The unexpressed, —
So wrought the charm of its elusive note

On us, who yearn in vain
To mock the pæan and the plain
Of tides that rise and fall with sweet mysterious rote.

Was it not well that the prophetic few,
So long inheritors of that high verse,
Dwelt in the mount alone, and haply knew
What stars rehearse?
But now with foolish cry the multitude
Awards at last the throne,
And claims thy cloudland for its own
With voices all untuned to thy melodious mood.

What joy it was to haunt some antique shade
Lone as thine echo, and to wreak my youth
Upon thy song, — to feel the throbs which made
Thy bliss, thy ruth, —
And thrill I knew not why, and dare to feel
Myself an heir unknown
To lands the poet treads alone
Ere to his soul the gods their presence quite reveal!

Even then, like thee, I vowed to dedicate
My powers to beauty; ay, but thou didst keep

The vow, whilst I knew not the afterweight
That poets weep,
The burthen under which one needs must bow,
The rude years envying
My voice the notes it fain would sing
For men belike to hear, as still they hear thee now.

Oh, the swift wind, the unrelenting sea!
They loved thee, yet they lured thee unaware
To be their spoil, lest alien skies to thee
Should seem more fair;
They had their will of thee, yet aye forlorn
Mourned the lithe soul's escape,
And gave the strand thy mortal shape
To be resolved in flame whereof its life was born.

Afloat on tropic waves, I yield once more
In age that heart of youth unto thy spell.
The century wanes: thy voice thrills as of yore
When first it fell.
Would that I too, so had I sung a lay
The least upborne of thine,
Had shared thy pain! Not so divine
Our light, as faith to chant the far auroral day.

On the Caribbean Sea
(Revisited 1892)

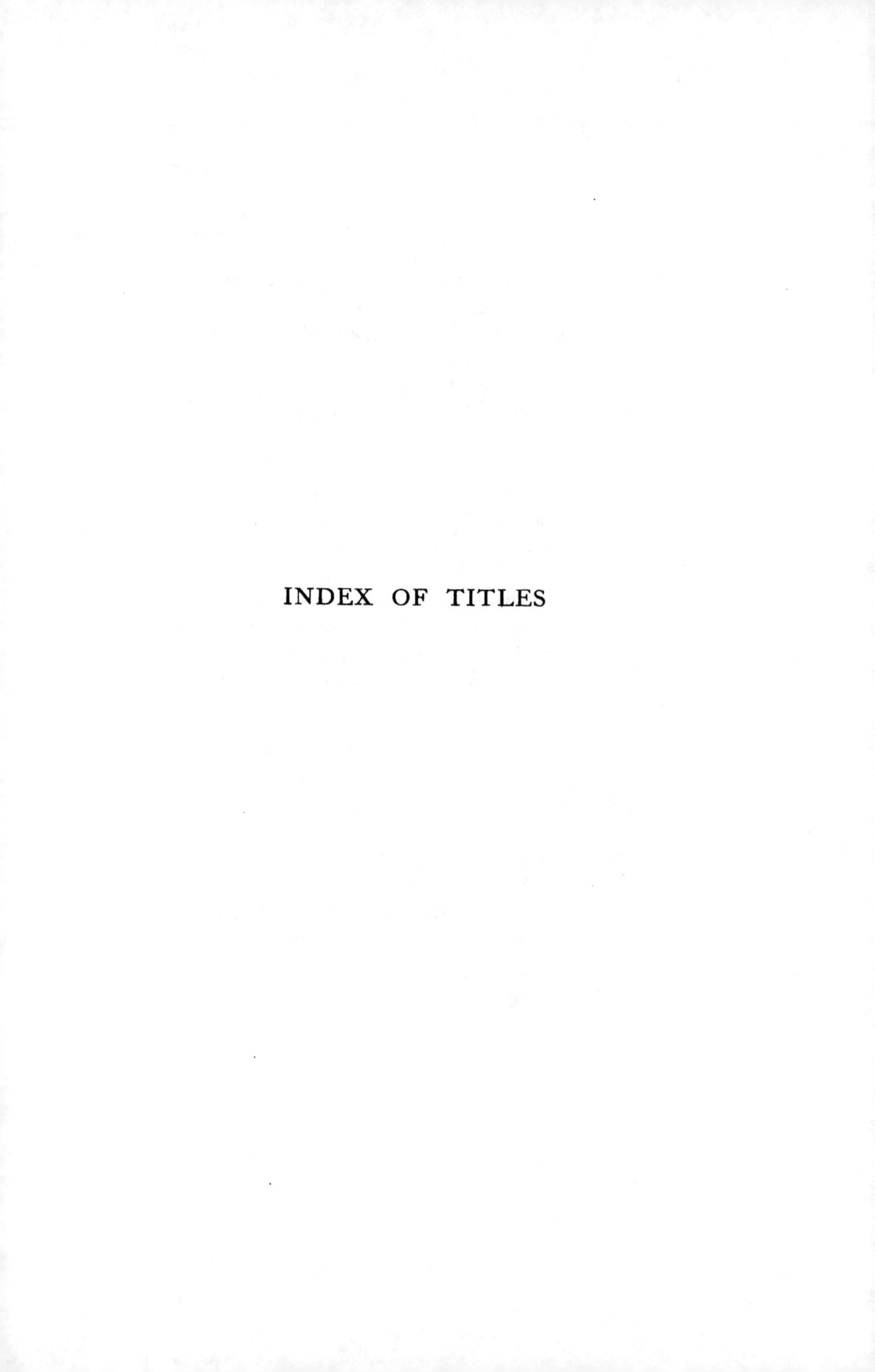

INDEX OF TITLES

INDEX OF TITLES

www.ingramcontent.com/pod-product-compliance
Lightning Source LLC
LaVergne TN
LVHW011204110826
845150LV00006B/1315

* 9 7 8 1 4 2 5 5 1 8 6 9 1 *